Antique Furniture Almanac

RONALD PEARSALL

Bloomsbury Books · London

First published by Lochar Publishing Ltd.
Moffat, Scotland DG10 9ED.

This edition published by Bloomsbury Books, an imprint of
The Godfrey Cave Group, 42 Bloomsbury Street, London, WC1B 3QJ,
under licence from Eric Dobby Publishing Ltd,
12 Warnford Road, Orpington, Kent BR6 6LW, 1993

Printed and bound in Great Britain by
BPCC Hazell Books Ltd

Member of BPCC Ltd

ISBN 1 85471 386 8

Contents

A
Short Guide
To
Buying
Furniture

There are three main ways of buying furniture – the auction room, the dealer, and privately, and each type of vendor can be endlessly divided. There are auctioneers who are models of probity, there are auctioneers who know nothing and care even less, and there are one or two crooks. But even when buying from the most reputable auction room, take note of the small print in the catalogue which invariably contains a 'let out' clause. If the buyer has bought what is known in the trade as a 'dog' it is too bad. He or she has made a choice and paid the money.

It is common sense to always view before buying, but even the oldest hands can get a rush of blood to the head and buy on spec. It is always worthwhile noting in the catalogue the price you are prepared to pay; always add £10 to the figure you have in mind – £210 instead of £200 to block out those who go up to a round figure.

If there is only one person in the auction room bidding against you it can be misleading; it may mean that the private buyers have dropped out and you are in competition with the spokesman of the dealers' ring. The dealers you know may be there in the auction room, and you may wonder why they are not bidding. You may win, because the dealers have to make a profit. But if you appear too enthusiastic, and are waving your catalogue as if it were a flag, the dealer may mischievously run you up so that you will pay far more for a piece than it is worth and will not trouble the dealers' ring again.

A house auction may fetch bigger prices than an auction in the sale room. There will always be private buyers for 'association' items, especially if the sale is taking place at a well-known country house. But a house auction held when the weather is bad and out-of-town buyers cannot get there can often yield bargains.

Buying from the highest echelon of dealers is the safest, but you will be paying 'top whack'. You will receive on request a detailed description of the item you have bought, and no dealer of the first rank would dream of misrepresentation. Further down the scale anything can happen. There may still be dealers who use fifteen watt bulbs in the recesses of their shops so that examination of their stock is dificult if not impossible. Many dealers operate on instinct. Their knowledge may be limited – sometimes deliberately so, in order that they don't get confused – and they rely on their feelings. And they may be wrong, so it is possible that they may be wildly out in their prices.

Be wary of middle-range dealers who do not price their goods, or dealers who use a code. Somtimes a code is used to prevent competitors from using price labels as a price guide; sometimes it is used so that the dealers can 'jack up' the price if they sense the credit-worthiness of a private buyer. Be wary too of self-styled experts who pontificate on prices. The question to be asked is this: would they personally pay the prices they put on certain pieces of furniture? The answer, too often, is no.

Boot sales and markets of all kinds can yield treasures, but not too often. One reason is that if there is any furniture worth 'pulling' the dealers have got there first, often waiting for sellers' vans, lorries and cars to arrive. Junk shops were once a happy hunting ground, but business rates have virtually killed them off and those that survive do not charge junk-shop prices.

Buying privately is splendid, provided you are buying privately and not from a dealer pretending to be a private vendor. A sign in a post office window 'Old chest for sale' may be the work of the dealer with a suspect piece on his hands who finds that it is easier to sell it from home rather than a shop. Advertising for certain types of furniture may work, but the odds are against it. Private sellers often prefer to sell anything worthwhile through the auction room, especially after the adverse publicity given to knockers and tinkers.

There are antiques and antiques of course. There are dealers with twenty years in the business who can't differentiate between eighteenth-century furniture and Edwardian versions of that furniture. There are ordinary people who simply haven't got a clue about their furniture, but if put to the question they would rate it far higher than it merits. Ordinary people are apt to own ordinary furniture.

With the popularity of price guides, some of them very good indeed, there is more knowledge about prices spread throughout the community than was once the case, but price guides rely heavily on auction prices, which in turn may have resulted from a peculiar combination of circumstances such as two determined collectors fighting it out in the sales room. So all valuations are speculative. Some furniture such as wine coolers or sofa tables are, in commonsense terms, too expensive. Other furniture, including old oak and wardrobes, are still cheap. But in all cases antique furniture will never cease to be a safe and profitable investment, a premier role it has taken over from property.

The
Story
Of
Furniture

Putting furniture into historical periods is a convenience. Furniture styles did not change when a new monarch came on the scene; they changed because a certain wood became fashionable, or because it began to be imported. They changed because of technical innovation, or because demands were different. In the large houses, living became more private and intimate. Society became less stiff – and the furniture shows it. Small tables for smaller rooms, occasional pieces of furniture to strew around a room instead of lining it all up along the walls.

There is nothing complex in furniture-making technology; there are four basic processes:

Carving
Planing
Turning using a revolving cutting edge (the lathe)
Sticking surfaces on (veneering)

When materials other than wood are used there is an additional process – moulding. This applies to papier mâché and modern plastics.

The periods shown in this book are English and American, but there are European parallels. These can be confusing. The French nomenclature is mainly concerned with the Louis periods; the most important Louis is Louis XIV (died 1715), the Sun King.

The overall story is simple:
Until the seventeenth century Britain, satisfied with its own often clumsy creations, lagged behind the rest of Europe. Only with the arrival of Charles II did foreign influences, especially Dutch and French, become truly important and oak lost its predominance as the main wood to use for furniture. The wood in fashion was walnut.

In America, the main colonizers were the British. They brought in their own ideas about furniture, and so did the Dutch, who settled in the Hudson valley, and the Germans, who occupied what is now Pennsylvania. There was almost no communication between these settlements. Furniture was basic, and often served dual purposes – as it did in medieval times. So the chest was something to sit on as well as a container. Furniture was rectangular, devoid of ornament, and solid. Not much of it remains. By the end of the seventeenth century American craftsmen were introducing their own ideas and motifs, but furniture was still essentially Anglo-Saxon. The highboy, a chest on a stand, was specifically American. There was now a merchant class in the US, with sophisticated demands. A characteristic of American country chairs was that they were often painted black or green.

In Britain in the eighteenth century, and with the arrival of mahogany, the position regarding Continental influences was reversed, and English designs were shamelessly copied, with regional variations and different woods, especially in Denmark, Sweden, and other countries with trading links with Britain. In America there were now cabinet makers the equal of Chippendale, and French influences were strong, especially in Philadelphia.

In the nineteenth century and after, styles became international. Britain had the Regency; the French had the Directoire and the Empire. Different names, but sharing common features, even common aspirations. Throughout Europe during the middle years of the nineteenth century there was a nostalgia for the past. In Britain it was the Gothic Revival, in France the Troubadour style, in Italy the Dantesque style, and America had its version of High Victorianism, often filtered from various sources, and mass-produced with an efficiency unknown in Britain and Europe. The '100-man shop' was commonplace in America.

Towards the end of the nineteenth century with the arrival of the movement known as *Art Nouveau* traditional styling went out of the window. Furniture seemed to be made through whims. It could be sinuous, spineless, and uncomfortable; it could be stark, angular – and equally uncomfortable. Naturally there was a reaction against this in the early twentieth century when there was a yearning for the restraint and good breeding of the eighteenth century, but in the 1920s there was another free-for-all – geometry-in-action versus cosy chintz. This seems to have lasted to the present day. If there is a common style which will be observable to future writers on furniture nobody has told us about it.   So on to the furniture periods:

MEDIEVAL (–1485). Very little furniture before about 1500 survives, and what we know of it depends on written and pictorial evidence. In illuminated manuscripts and the like the most important piece of furniture is the throne. Furniture was not regarded highly. It was portable and carried from castle to castle as the well-to-do moved about the country. As carpentry is not a difficult craft, no doubt there were men in the towns and villages who could create simple furniture for practical use amongst the vast masses of the population.

TUDOR (1485–1603).The ruggedness of the furniture is often at odds with what we think we know of the period. Furniture was still not very important and was used as an accessory to the colourful cushions, embroideries and hangings. Decoration was predominantly carved, and new types of craftsmen such as the joiner came into being, responsible for joined (or 'joint') work (chairs, chests, doors, and tables). This was often furniture called 'dormant', meant to stay where it was and not moved from place to place. The main pieces of furniture were the chest, the various cupboards, tables, and stools. The draw-leaf table came into being about 1550. The panel-backed chair was the typical model for two centuries. It was only used by the superior folk; the common man (and woman) used stools. The use of a framework to raise the bedding above the ground was not commonly practised until the early seventeenth century, so the four-poster bed was not universal.   Continental furniture was far more sophisticated, and was often imported. With Elizabeth on the throne furniture became increasingly self-assertive and imposing, and upholstered furniture became fashionable.

JACOBEAN (1603–25). Oak was still the most important wood during the reign of James I, but it was treated differently, with less emphasis on the massive and over-blown, and there was more skill in the use of elaborate turning. Hanging cupboards became popular, and so were low wide chairs and settees in the form of two chairs side by side. Much of the furniture was undramatic, but colour was provided by the vogue for rich and exotic carpets which were used as bed covers and hangings as well as to walk upon. In America communities were isolated, and furniture was functional, made from local woods such as hickory and maple little used in Britain and Europe.

CAROLEAN (1625–49). Charles I was a cultivated man, and strove to improve Britain's taste in furniture. Furniture, still predominantly oak, became more refined, and gateleg tables became increasingly popular as the practice of dining at small tables became common. Chests 'with drawers' were becoming chests of drawers, though in the early stages these drawers were concealed behind doors. There was more adventure, with the use of inlay of bone and mother-of-pearl, and the introduction of exotic woods.

COMMONWEALTH (1649–60). Under Oliver Cromwell life was austere, and the furniture reflected this. Much of the furniture which the Cromwellians thought decadent was destroyed. Carving was frowned upon as being out of tune with the new age, but modest turning, especially bobbin turning, was permitted. An interesting feature was the use of leather in chairs. There is not much fun in Commonwealth furniture. America escaped this clamping down on comfort, pursuing their own ideas, often more innovative than those in Britain.

RESTORATION (1660–89). When he came to the throne in 1660, Charles II brought with him new ideas of furniture and fittings from the continent, lighter, more elegant, and with walnut the favoured wood and not oak. Walnut was used in veneers as well as the solid, and was also very popular in America, not as a fashion from Britain but discovered by the inhabitants, finding walnut ideal for turning and carving. Perhaps walnut would have been a passing fad had the Great Fire of London not happened in 1666, destroying not only the houses but the contents, and encouraging those replacing their furniture to go for walnut. The main stylistic influence came from Holland, with floral marquetry, ornate chests of drawers, cabinets, and caned chairs. The bookcase appeared. A wide variety of inlays were used including ebony and tortoiseshell. Gilt furniture became fashionable, and fittings of iron were replaced by those of brass. There was also a vogue for *Chinoiserie* (furniture in the Chinese style or what was imagined to be the Chinese style), and lacquered furniture. A desire for comfort resulted in increased use of upholstery and the evolution of furniture such as the day bed. Away from urban centres oak and country woods continued to be used, regardless of high fashion.

WILLIAM AND MARY (1689–1702). There was an increasing emphasis on comfort and lightness, heavy Dutch influences slowly being replaced by more elegant French styles, in part due to the immigration of Hugenot refugees from France. Walnut was still in favour for furniture, as was lacquer, and several new forms of furniture were introduced such as the swing toilet mirror and the bureau. Looking glasses were very popular, and there was a great variety of chairs, including upholstered winged armchairs. Caned furniture was popular. A new type of chair appeared, with a narrow back of curved outline, a vase- or fiddle-shaped central splat, and cabriole front legs, similar to those used in France. The first tables specifically made for card playing appeared, and dressing tables, either of the knee-hole type or with drawers on short legs, were fashionable, especially among women. In America, as well as the highboy, in walnut or sometimes laquered black, a particular type of slant-top desk made its appearance. Furniture remained functional, but the importing of ceramics and other treasures created a need for display tables and other pieces.

QUEEN ANNE (1702–14). Typified by the wide use of the cabriole leg, simplification, the decline of lacquer and carving, and the first signs of the classicism that was to make its mark on the later part of the century. The claw-and-ball foot was introduced about 1710, partly replacing hoofed and scrolled feet. Chairs were more comfortable, as were settees, sometimes called love seats.. The fashion for panelled rooms meant that cupboards could be built into the walls. During the walnut period (1690–1730) oak was still used, especially by country makers. Burr-walnut veneer was particularly popular during the Queen Anne period, and some chests of drawers were mounted on stands. The construction of cased furniture (chests of drawers etc) was also more elegant, with finer dovetailing. Bracket feet replaced ball or bun feet. English furniture had come of age. It was as good as any in Europe. American furniture of this period was based on English models, somewhat simplified. Chairs were smaller. There was increasing regional variation.

GEORGIAN (1714–1811). In 1720 there was a walnut famine. Walnut was an indigenous French wood, and the authorities placed an embargo on its export, and supplies in the English American colonies were insufficient. Mahogany was the answer, first noted more than a hundred years earlier but not greatly used. Walnut furniture was made until about 1760 but the eighteenth century is dominated by mahogany, and by four stylists.

THE WILLIAM KENT OR PALLADIAN STYLE. William Kent (1685–1748) was an architect who went to Rome in 1710 and returned to promote classical styles. His interest was in the rich and only the rich. His furniture is on a massive and often brooding scale. Just right for a hundred-bedroomed country house.

THE ADAM STYLE. Dating from 1758 when Robert Adam returned from four years' architectural study in Rome with new ideas. Not naturalistic and frivolous like the fashionable French style, not solemn and ponderous, but based on motifs and designs he had seen in ancient baths, villas, and tombs, such as corn husks, bell-flowers, shells, honeysuckle and foliage scrolls. The hall marks of the Adam style are sophistication and refinement; these could become tired and trivial. He established the dining-room sideboard as a major piece of furniture.

THE CHIPPENDALE STYLE. Open to influences from all over the world, the further away the better, Chippendale (1718–79) is a shadowy figure. What he wrote about was more important than what he did. His pattern books feature fretwork , lacquer-work, pagoda shapes, Gothic motifs, and he also adapted pretty-pretty forms in a new and adventurous way, twisting French designs so that they fitted in with English furniture. He also took over Adam's ideas.

THE HEPPLEWHITE STYLE. Hepplewhite (died 1786) was not so concerned with furniture for the grand houses. His furniture was domestic, elegant, graceful. Typical is the Hepplewhite chair with oval, heart and shield backs; he is especially associated with the Prince of Wales's feathers motif. Probably the most refined of all the furniture designers, always in keeping, never boisterous.

THE SHERATON STYLE. Sheraton was strongly influenced by Adam but he also evolved new French-like decorative motifs such as the lattice and lozenge, and it was the richness and delicacy of French furniture that appealed to him, plus a fondness for strong perpendicular lines, as in chair backs. With less formality in the home, there was a demand for less ceremonial furniture, and Sheraton was at his best in informal pieces, though some of his designs were bizarre, anticipating his later derangement.

There was no culture lag between Britain and America, but Queen Anne furniture continued to be popular in America long after it had become outmoded in Britain. Chippendale became an important influence in the US. An interesting American piece was the 'block-front' bookcase or chest, made in three vertical blocks with the centre one recessed. The American War of Independence delayed the introduction of neo-Classicism, but when it did this type of furniture – and architecture – was held to represent the aspirations of George Washington and his successors.

REGENCY (1811–20). Strictly speaking 1811–20, but generally understood to cover the years from 1793 to 1830, sometimes beyond, depending on taste. There was a reaction against spindliness and fragility, and an emphasis on straight clean lines, typified by the chiffonier. The main show wood was rosewood, though mahogany and satinwood continued to be used. Marquetry was unfashionable, and brass inlay was in vogue. Much of the furniture was powerful, and there was a taste for strong often brutal contrasts. Egyptian, Chinese, Greek and Roman styles were popular, all treated in a no-nonsense way, not only in Britain and Europe but America as well, on its way to an unbelievable prosperity now that it was independent.

WILLIAM IV (1830–7). The most important thing to happen during William IV's brief and not very spectacular reign was the publication of the influential *Encyclopaedia of Cottage, Farm and Villa Architecture and Furniture by* J.C. Loudon in 1833 which set out the guide lines for the future. Loudon named the four prevailing styles as *Grecian, Gothic, Elizabethan* and *Louis*

Quatorze. His readers nodded approvingly. This is what they liked too. He gave respectability to the revival of old styles of furniture. Some would say he had a lot to answer for.

VICTORIAN (1837–1901). There was no break in tradition when Queen Victoria ascended the throne, and Regency designs remained popular, coarsened and altered. But ideas were simmering, a fondness for show, complexity, obvious value for money, experiment, and glitter. There was also a nostalgic look back at older styles, especially Gothic, which was restructured for a new prosperous age. Modern technology made it possible to produce fussy and over-decorated articles at little cost. This was especially true in America; the furniture workshop became a factory. Decoration and surface flourish seemed to be all, but exhibition pieces did not represent furniture in the average home. This could be modest and unostentatious or ridiculous and pretentious. 'Old money' scorned the new fangled styles, and continued to use eighteenth-century and earlier furniture (that is why so much of it is still available today). Manufacturers were always striving for novelty – a chair was made from coal – plundering the past for ideas, and searching for new stimulants, such as the Japanese furniture in the exhibition of 1862.

EDWARDIAN (1901–10). The last decades of the nineteenth century saw the emergence of Art Nouveau, signalling a total rejection of the past, though, also in reaction against the excesses of the Victorian period, there was a return to eighteenth-century-type furniture superbly made in mahogany and satinwood. Somewhat out of the main stream was 'arty' furniture of the 'country cottage' type, with a preference for light-coloured woods, waxed not varnished, simple and inexpensive or, if the manufacturer was fashionable, simple and expensive.

GEORGE V (1910–36). There was no general style during the reign of George V. After World War I the demand was for easy comfort. In America there was a yearning for the old colonial furniture with simple lines and little fuss. The absence of domestic servants led to a desire for clean surfaces needing a minimum of dusting, so functional furniture was dull. But in 1925 an exhibition in Paris introduced geometric, brightly coloured, streamlined and thoroughly modern furniture onto the scene. This was known as *Art Deco*. Most ordinary people saw it in Hollywood films or in cinema foyers, and if they did buy it it was fitted out with razzle-dazzle veneers, smoked and silvered glass, and chrome. This co-existed with 'fitness-for-function' furniture, sparked off in Europe and especially Germany, Scandinavia and Holland; this looked like office furniture and still does.

WORLD WAR II (1939–45). World War I had had no effect on furniture design. During World War II there was a determined effort to make furniture functional. This was called *Utility* furniture, and it was the only kind manufacturers were allowed to make. Plywood was much used, as were the 'sensible' woods such as oak. There was little or no decoration. It had a great effect on post-war furniture designers. *Austerity* was a key word well into the 1950s, and the furniture matched the mood, whether or not it was timidly decked out with plastic. Austerity furniture was a British phenomenon. It is often forgotten that the British war effort was the most systematically geared of them all and discomfort was rated a moral quality. In America in 1940 a revolutionary type of furniture made its appearance, a one-piece chair of shell form made of veneer and glue laminated in a mould; in America in 1948 a moulded shell chair of plastic and fibreglass made its appearance.

POST-WAR YEARS (1945 –). As with the age of George V there is no generally accepted style. It is rather a question of picking and choosing. The consumer-orientated society gets what it thinks it wants, or rather what the advertisers think it should have. If there is a classic furniture style, no-one with any qualifications to make a judgement has seen it, and it is not surprising that people with taste prefer the furniture of a bygone age – in fact, almost anything pre-war. Thus the appeal of antique furniture. In view of the current vacuum in furniture design, no wonder that the demand for antique furniture is not likely to dry up.

Furniture Guide

Prices of antique furniture are, of course, flexible. There is no Retail Price Maintenance nor ever has been. It has been decided to use a system of coding to reflect the range of prices, mostly the prices made in an auction room.

A		—	£500
B	£500	—	£1500
C	£1500	—	£3000
D	£3000	—	£5000
E	£5000	+	

Piece:	**AMERICAN NURSING CHAIR**
Material:	Mahogany
Dimensions:	2ft 8in high, 2ft wide
Period:	*c.*1870
Value:	A

POINTS TO LOOK FOR: There is nothing to distinguish this chair from its English equivalent, reflecting the fact that middle-class culture in the US was little different from in Britain. It is definitely American because it is accompanied by a bill from a New York furniture retailer, and this may nudge the value into band B even though it is quite an ordinary chair without a great deal to commend it save comfort. To have any value an easy chair of this type should be in good condition with the upholstery undamaged and if possible original, as in this instance.

HISTORY: The title of nursing chair may have been wished on this type of furniture by auctioneers. The main features are the low seat and the absence of arms, making it easy to feed a baby. The concept of chairs for every conceivable purpose was enthusiastically embraced by the Victorians, though it was anticipated in the eighteenth century especially by the French women who dominated salon life. In Victorian middle-class families with a large number of children such chairs were commonplace and were it not for the wholesale destruction of Victoriana after 1900 there would be many more about.

Piece:	**ART DECO DRESSING TABLE**
Material:	Laminated wood
Dimensions:	2ft 6in high, 3ft 8in wide
Period:	*c.*1930
Value:	A

POINTS TO LOOK FOR: Art Deco has been collected now for more than twenty years, but straightforward items such as this without the kudos of a maker's name are still largely disregarded especially in the provinces. Many of the mirrors attached to dressing tables are hideous and completely out of proportion, and as the bases are often of high quality it has become a practice to remove the mirror tops and turn them into a kind of writing table, often successfully. As veneer was wafer thin it has a tendency to peel, especially on curved surfaces.

HISTORY: The dressing table provided a piece of furniture custom-made for women, and the forms altered dramatically throughout the years from the kneehole type, through the sideboard type of the early nineteenth century, through remarkably ugly Victorian specimens into the glittering and flashy Art Deco dressing table. Ideally suited to the jazz age and self satisfaction, with triple mirrors that could be adjusted to any angle and a multitude of drawers and compartments for the new aids to beauty. As such it did its job well and is not to be sneered at.

Piece:	**ART DECO SOFA**
Material:	Laminated wood
Dimensions:	3ft high, 6ft wide
Period:	1930s
Value:	£100-£500

POINTS TO LOOK FOR: Because style was all, looks were more important than construction, though this sofa is a quality piece. Original fabrics, such as the popular uncut moquette, are a major plus, though modern velour, as here, is acceptable. The wood used is often plywood (five-ply) veneered, often with exotic and expensive woods, figured walnut being the favourite. Veneer on plywood tends to peel, and if the veneer is highly ornate (and being modern it will be wafer-thin) it will perhaps fall into bits. The presence of a maker's label (often of celluloid or other plastic) is important. It may need to be searched for.

HISTORY: Art Deco was the fashionable style of the 1920s and 1930s, sometimes known as the Odeon style or the Modern Style, in which streamlining, smooth surfaces and fitness-for-function were greatly valued. A better title would be the cinema foyer style. There were favourite motifs, such as zigzags, sunbursts, and geometrical designs, often deriving from the art of the time. Chainstore Art Deco is very cheap, especially in the provinces. £10 could, in fact, buy something of quality, an antique of the future.

Piece:	**BACHELOR CHEST**
Material:	Red walnut
Dimensions:	2ft 6in high, 2ft wide
Period:	*c.*1745
Value:	D

POINTS TO LOOK FOR: A feature of this chest is that each of the four drawers has a a centre decorative escutcheon with a keyhole. These could be misleading, and may not indicate a lock for every drawer, but of all metal attachments to furniture locks have the most tendency to go wrong, so make certain that at least the drawers are not jammed. The handles look right, but are they in too good a condition for a chest that has had a fair amount of damage? The front right bracket foot has been hopelessly repaired, there is a sliver missing above the bottom drawer, and there is an ugly mark at the side, which could have been easily remedied. However, these are acceptable in a piece of this period.

HISTORY: This is a transitional chest of drawers made towards the end of the walnut period, but bearing none of the trademarks of walnut. It is walnut, in fact, used as mahogany, which may indicate that it is a country piece, further emphasised by its stolid no-nonsense character. It is known as a bachelor chest for one reason and one reason only – the so-called 'brushing slide' which slides out above the drawers and below the moulded top.

Piece:	**BALLOON-BACK CHAIR**
Material:	Mahogany
Dimensions:	3ft high, 1ft 8in wide
Period:	*c*.1860
Value:	A

Points to look for: The date is speculative, as this type of chair was made for many decades, and there are a number of variations in the backs ranging from a flattened to a full oval. Quality also varies enormously and the heavier types, as in the illustration, served as standard dining chair. The back was often made in two parts and in this example the join can be clearly seen. Legs varied, from cabriole legs in the French Louis XV style to slender turned and fluted legs, and the seats could be over-stuffed or drop-in. Mahogany was the preferred wood, followed by walnut.

History: The balloon-back chair was a classic design, and many criticisms of Victorian excesses in furniture design can be deflected by mentioning the balloon back, which first made a tentative entry in the 1840s, though not yet in a fully developed form. Very popular from the 1960s, when Victorian furniture began to be appreciated and exported in quantity, the balloon back was made in great quantities and prices are still reasonable. A high-quality set is often far more serviceable than an eighteenth-century ensemble costing many times as much.

Piece:	**BONHEUR DU JOUR**
Material:	Walnut
Dimensions:	4ft 7in high, 2ft 11in wide
Period:	*c*.1860
Value:	C–D

Points to look for: The wide price valuation band indicates that this is the type of furniture certain people cannot resist. It is a private piece not a 'trade' piece, usually of superb quality because it is a luxury item of limited use. The fittings vary from item to item. The example illustrated has a bureau facility and two velvet-lined display cabinets. Others have drawers and a bank of shelves at the back, with a flat writing surface. Each example has to be examined on its merits. Look for quality inlay, carving, the extra touches of a master craftsman for whom nothing was too much trouble.

History: Introduced from France towards the end of the eighteenth century as a ladies' writing table, the bonheur du jour, whatever the 'good hour of the day' may be, was never Anglicized, though a variant of it was called a cheveret. It was never vulgarised, not even in the 1860s. Some examples have built-in mirrors, others painted decoration, and satinwood was often used. A brass gallery was an optional extra. The very best examples of the bonheur du jour command well in excess of £10,000. Edwardian examples, sometimes signed, are among the leaders.

Piece:	**BOUILLOTTE**
Material:	Mahogany with brass gallery
Dimensions:	2ft 6in high, 1ft 6in across
Period:	*c.*1880
Value:	C

POINTS TO LOOK FOR: Centre or occasional tables were made in many varieties, and each one has to be looked at on its merits. The example illustrated is French and was made for the game of bouillotte; some centre tables have marbled tops, but other materials can include mosaic, ivory inlay, marquetry, porcelain plaques, baize, even silk. Centre tables can be round, oval, square, octagonal, or oblong. They can be set on legs, pedestals, end supports or tripods. They can have a definite purpose or none at all. As with other furniture, the craftsmanship and style is more important than the dazzle of glittering surfaces; an intricate surface pattern needs to be examined closely to ensure that there is no renovation or that a plain surface has not been 'improved'.

HISTORY: Centre tables became popular when everyday life became less formal in the eighteenth century, and furniture was spread throughout a room rather than around it. The popularity of walnut and mahogany in Britain also helped — it was difficult to make pretty occasional tables of oak. In the nineteenth century the fondness for clutter created a demand for fancy tables of all descriptions.

Piece:	**BREAKFRONT BOOKCASE**
Material:	Satinwood with marquetry
Dimensions:	7ft 10in high, 8ft 4in wide
Period:	*c*.1880
Value:	E

Points to look for: The breakfront bookcase is at the top of the antique furniture tree. It is not likely to be 'come across' and would rarely appear outside a top auction room or a high-quality antique shop. The illustrated example, although late Victorian, made £16,500. Why? Because of its superb quality in every respect. Its success emphasises that furniture of all periods can make big money. Bookcases with so much surface decoration need going over carefully, making certain that all the marquetry is intact, inlay perfect. In earlier examples minor repairs are acceptable, but not in something of this age or quality.

History: The bookcase was first intrduced in 1666, mentioned by the diarist Pepys. Early specimens were oak, fairly plain and robust. In the eighteenth century bookshelves were built into panelled walls, but some gentlemen preferred large free-standing bookcases in their libraries. Fancy bookcases in the extravagant Gothic style became popular, with lots of arches and pinnacles, but the breakfront bookcase, called so because it is in three sections, the centre section protruding, remained the classic.

Piece:	**BUREAU**
Material:	Mahogany
Dimensions:	3ft 7in high, 3ft 9in wide
Period:	*c.*1760
Value:	D

POINTS TO LOOK FOR: The quality of a bureau can be gauged by the fitted interior, which can be a marvel of craftsmanship with secret drawers, elegant stepping and superb detail, such as the provision of pillars for the central section. Sometimes bureaux have been revived too much; walnut should have different shades of colour. Restorers sometimes clean off to a single light brown. See that the feet are in period; bracket feet are vulnerable to damp and ill usage, and may have been replaced, or bracket feet may have replaced bun feet. Take out the bottom drawer and look for unexplained holes. Did the bureau have a top on? Look for signs on the top – holes, discolouration, patches.

HISTORY: The first writing furniture was a box with a sloping lid. A stand was later fitted, with the flap of the revamped box coming over and forming a writing surface, supported by overlapping the base, pull-out slides, or a 'gate' opening in the centre. The space beneath the desk could be used, filling in with drawers. Thus the bureau. Designs and woods conformed to fashion – oak, walnut, mahogany. Country makers used local woods, and their fitted interiors were simple and uncluttered.

Piece:	**BUREAU BOOKCASE**
Material:	Walnut
Dimensions:	7ft 9in high, 3ft 6in wide
Period:	*c*.1710
Value:	E

POINTS TO LOOK FOR: No-one has come up with a formula for effectively reproducing a period bureau bookcase of this quality, and anyone who is taken in by an imitation must be a rare bird indeed and hardly to be trusted out with a ten-pound note. This particular specimen is in marvellous condition, and if there is any degree of restoration it is difficult to see, though a degree of wear and tear is acceptable, which might appear in the vulnerable bureau fittings hidden behind the fall front. Some bureaux bookcases have slides for candlesticks, but their absence is not alarming.

HISTORY: The bureau bookcase, introduced at the very beginning of the eighteenth century, is the essential antique, although it went out of use in the nineteenth century when good looks were not enough and the scribbling fraternity, men and women, looked for something more useful, its prestige since World War II has gradually increased. Throughout its history there was always a temptation to cram into it far too much, often in the grandest style, and the bureau fittings were often models of intricacy with the obligatory secret compartments.

Piece:	**CABINET**
Materials:	Satinwood
Dimensions:	5ft 4in high, 3ft 6in wide
Period:	*c.*1790
Value:	E

Points to look for: The English cabinet is so different from its European equivalents that it might be a totally different piece of furniture. The late eighteenth-century cabinet-makers made marvellous use of unusual woods as inlay. Boxwood was often used, as here, but purple wood, sometimes known as purple heart, is rare. It came from Brazil, and turned to brown from purple on exposure to the air, was hard and heavy, and not dissimilar to rosewood. The material in the oval panels, protected by wire grills, is not fabric, but painted panels imitating silk, an extremely unusual feature in English furniture.

History: Cabinets were important, often of marvellous quality and, being prestige pieces, were unlike other furniture of their periods, and as early as 1598 a German traveller, Paul Hentzer, commented on a superb cabinet he had seen at Hampton Court. Cabinets were used to show off the owners' treasures, and magnificent cabinets of olive and kingwood were owned by Charles II and William III. By 1790 even fine cabinets were cheap. The basic cost of a cabinet was £3. 8s (£3.40)–£4.16s (£4.80) (excluding the cost of wood, 'extras', and profit).

Piece:	**CANTERBURY**
Material:	Walnut
Dimensions:	1ft 8in high, 1ft 8in wide
Period:	*c*.1860
Value:	B

POINTS TO LOOK FOR: The partitions of Canterburies are often in the form of fretwork, which are very vulnerable to damage. Check that there are no pieces missing, or if repairs have been carried out. This is sometimes difficult as the partitions are often set close together. Make sure that a damaged partition has not been taken out. There will be clues to this on the base – unexplained patches or changes of wood colour. Even more important is that it really is a period Canterbury and not a piece made up from a drawer with added partitions and feet.

HISTORY: The name Canterbury comes from a piece of movable furniture liked by an unknown archbishop. It appeared in the eighteenth century as an atlas stand and even a food trolley, but from about 1800 it was established as a holder for music. It was made in all woods, including lacquer and bamboo, as well as papier mâché, and was often very intricate (and ugly), sometimes incorporating a top with a gallery. Eighteenth-century examples, especially in satinwood (rare), can be worth £4000, an absurd price for such an object considering the ease with which it was made.

Piece:	**CELLARET**
Material:	Mahogany with brass banding
Dimensions:	2ft 4in high, 3ft wide.
Period:	Late eighteenth century
Value:	B the pair

POINTS TO LOOK FOR: Cellarets are far more expensive than the modest amount of workmanship involved in their construction merits, and they are extensively faked, especially the octagonal types (oval or round cellarets are more difficult to make). Many were fitted with castors (sometimes of leather, usually brass) and these should be examined for signs of wear. Any brass fittings or banding should be chunky not wafer thin, and the handles should look in keeping with the general style – not too large.

HISTORY: The cellaret was a box, often on legs or a stand, with a waterproof liner, popular from the eighteenth century to about 1830, a wine cooler where the wine was stored or chilled before use at the table, a half-way house between cellar and wine glass.   Mostly made from mahogany, though there are Sheraton types in satinwood inlaid with tulipwood. Wine was also kept cooled in the side cupboards of sideboards (often believed to be dressing tables because of their great elegance). Cellarets were prestige items, indicating that the owners knew all about wine. Now obsolete, they serve as drawing-room decorative items or conversation pieces.

Piece:	**CHEST OF DRAWERS**
Material:	Walnut and marquetry
Dimensions:	3ft 3in high, 3ft 5in wide
Period:	*c.*1710
Value:	C

POINTS TO LOOK FOR: After 1670 bottom runners appeared, to make drawers easier to open, useful as a dating guide. In the eighteenth century no drawers fully fitted the space available (to give ventilation). Walnut became fashionable about 1680, mahogany about 1740, bringing new shapes – bow fronts, serpentine, etc. Up to 1770 the grain in the drawer bottoms tended to run front to back, later side to side. If any top surface veneer looks too new or if there are three small drawers on top it may be that the chest of drawers was a chest on stand or chest on chest. These did not have veneers which no-one would see.

HISTORY: The chest of drawers is a direct descendant of the ordinary chest, the most important piece of furniture in the medieval household. A chest with a drawer appeared in the seventeenth century, and it was reasoned that a combination of drawers would be a good idea. Chests of drawers could be simple or enormously ornate; the continental equivalent, the commode, could be breathtaking. In the nineteenth century chests of drawers became massive; there was a reaction against this about 1900, leading to neat smaller pieces in oak.

Piece:	**CHEST ON CHEST**
Material:	Walnut
Dimensions:	5ft 8in high, 3ft 3in wide
Period:	*c.*1720
Value:	E

POINTS TO LOOK FOR: Colour is more important than construction in determining value, the figuration of this chest on chest is magnificent. Here there is no question that it is all of a piece, not a 'marriage', using two disparate pieces of furniture to make something else. Our ancestors were shorter than we are, and the top was never seen except by the diligent dusting servant. Bracket feet, made more decorative about 1740 using the ogee shape, is the norm, and bun feet would indicate a Victorian 'improvement'.

HISTORY: Chest on chest, tallboy, chest of drawers in two stages, they are all the same, and within the form there was room for considerable variation. Introduced early in the eighteenth century, suitable for both walnut and mahogany, it fell out of favour in the nineteenth when the eminent cabinet-maker George Smith observed the disagreeable necessity 'of getting on to chairs to place anything in the upper drawers.' The cornice was usually straight and hollow, though a broken pediment was sometimes used. The inlaid sunburst motif in the bottom drawer was a sign of true quality. The bow-fronted Hepplewhite-style examples of 1780 onwards are less expensive.

Piece:	**CHIFFONIER**
Material:	Rosewood and gilt metal
Dimensions:	4ft high, 4ft 5in wide
Period:	*c.*1815
Value:	D

POINTS TO LOOK FOR: Check that the brass gallery, inlay and any other decorative devices are intact. Brass trellis work is not difficult to repair, but restoration can always be detected. See that the feet are in keeping – Regency chiffoniers such as this may have been fitted with bun feet when they became fashionable; look for unexplained screw holes in the base. If there is a mirror back it should be in good condition. Crackling and a brownish tinge indicates deterioration which may get worse. If too bad, replace. As chiffoniers were back-to-the-wall pieces, the back may look unfinished. It is easier to see from the back if any upper structure is original or an addition.

HISTORY: The chiffonier has a muddled history. Some experts refuse to recognise it, classifying it as a side cabinet. In its commonly understood form it is a Regency piece with an upper shelf or shelves, grille front, often curtained with silk, sometimes with a brass gallery and brass inlay. As Regency chiffoniers are popular, they have often been made up from Victorian sideboards by taking out the arched front panels, squaring up, and replacing with a silk-backed grille.

Piece:	**CHINESE EXPORT DESK**
Material:	Amboyna and ebony
Dimensions:	2ft 6in high, 4ft 1in wide
Period:	*c.*1820
Value:	C

POINTS TO LOOK FOR: Made in China for export, perhaps to America, the criteria that governs British, American, and European furniture still hold. The main one is the quality of workmanship. How would one tell that this was Chinese? One of the clues is the feet. The handles which lie flush with their brass plates would denote that this is out of the usual; inset handles were customary in campaign furniture, not in prestige furniture vulnerable to damage in transit. Both the top and the base protrude. This would not happen in military furniture. The double-decker top is curious. Is it a desk? Is it a dressing table? It would certainly be uncomfortable to use.

HISTORY: With the opening up of China by explorers, entrepreneurs, and missionaries, porcelain, fabrics, and lacquer work were the first major exports to the west. Furniture used by the Chinese was traditionally fine and simple, but they had the ability to provide anything the barbarians of the west wanted, often using designs provided by the importers. If the foreigners wanted exotic veneers, they could have them.

Piece:	**CHIPPENDALE CHAIR.**
Material:	Mahogany
Dimensions:	3ft 2in high 2ft wide
Period:	*c.*1760
Value:	E set of six

Points to look for: Chippendale chairs have been reproduced, often with the best of intentions, since Chippendale died. Victorian reproductions often fool the experts, but sometimes the makers altered the proportions, making the seats smaller, overdoing the ornament or carrying it out clumsily. Look for the well-worn look of old faded mahogany, avoid glitter and shine, look for genuine signs of wear. The example above is square legged in the Gothic style, but Chippendale also used cabriole legs. Examine the union of legs and seat, look for repairs, which may be cleverly carried out. A broken splat can be almost invisibly repaired.

History: Thomas Chippendale (1718–79) designed furniture rather than made it. His *The Gentleman and Cabinet-Maker's Director* (1754) was the first comprehensive pattern book for furniture. His output was small. Cabinet-makers, not only in London but throughout Britain, made their furniture from his designs, with their own variations. Consequently there is a wide variety. Chippendale had several styles, the most important being Gothic and Chinese. His son carried on the tradition.

Piece:	**COFFER**
Material:	Oak
Dimensions:	2ft 1in high, 3ft 11in wide
Period:	*c*.1660
Value:	C

Points to look for: The first task of anyone looking at a chest or coffer (the terms are often interchangeable though the word coffer is most popularly used for a container for money) is to ascertain if the decoration is in keeping with the piece or added later, to improve the looks of a plain chest or to increase its value. Often fakers make the mistake of making the carving too primitive or overloading it. Fakers also shun hard work, the decoration on this chest would defeat most, not the fairly light scratch carving of the plant fronds but the deeply incised lozenge shapes with their tricky moulded borders.

History: The first coffer was a hollowed-out tree trunk, and as the coffer was almost the only piece of furniture many people had to store clothes or other goods it was made well into the modern age, almost without change, with or without the addition of a drawer (the mule chest). Not surprisingly there are many about, and prices reflect this. Repeating geometric ornament was popular, as were initials. It was considered a good idea by fakers to add a date, often totally at odds with the wood used or the style of the coffer.

Piece:	**COMMODE**
Material:	Mahogany and marquetry
Dimensions:	3ft 6in high, 3ft wide
Period:	*c.*1910
Value:	C

POINTS TO LOOK FOR: Gone are the days when Edwardian furniture was ignored while Australia and the US went berserk over ghastly pieces of Victoriana, and the fact that this commode sold for £2,200 several years ago indicates a decided change. However, condition is all important and the kind of damage acceptable in the eighteenth-century piece is not acceptable in Edwardian furniture. With extravagant marquetry every section needs examined to make certain a repair has not been carried out. A characteristic of the commode was legs were integrated with the carcase.

HISTORY: The commode was an important article of furniture in Europe, less so in Britain where the name was given to a chamber pot receptacle. It evolved from the chest, and the name seems to have been first used in 1708. Some references mention them as 'tables with deep drawers', on the continent it was another name for a chest of drawers. Early Georgian commodes were highly decorated but lacked the unity of French models, and later eighteenth-century commodes were often rich in hand-painted decoration. Had this Edwardian piece been other than a commode the marquetry would have been less elaborate.

Piece:	**CONSOLE TABLE**
Material:	Amboyna with plaques, brass inlay, and marble top
Dimensions:	3ft 2in high, 5ft 5in wide
Period:	*c.*1780
Value:	E.

POINTS TO LOOK FOR: Furniture of this quality is only available from dealers of the highest credibility or from top auction rooms, and this alone guarantees it. However, even in exalted circles *caveat emptor* may apply. Complicated brass inlay involving convoluted patterns needs going over inch by inch, if necessary with a magnifying glass. Be wary of marble tops. Striations, accepted as part of the figure, may be incipient breaks. As the Wedgwood plaque is vulnerable, examine closely, though plaques of this quality are almost impossible to repair convincingly.

HISTORY: The introduction of the console table, originally called a 'clap' table and French inspired, dates from the early years of the eighteenth century. In early days a bracket construction was used with an eagle's outstretched wings acting as support. The console table is associated with the name of Robert Adam (1728–92) and was primarily a show object made to impress the lesser folk. The marble was imported (expensively – and all the visitors knew it) from Italy though reconstituted marble (scagliola) or alabaster were used as cheaper substitutes.

Piece:	**CORNER CUPBOARD**
Material:	Pine
Dimensions:	7ft high, 2ft 9in wide
Period:	1991
Value:	A

Points to look for: As this was made recently it might seem odd to place it in an almanac of antiques, but it is the kind of useful article in the traditional style which lends itself to being distressed and made to look old. Pine is a soft wood which can be convincingly aged. Pieces were often painted, especially in America and Europe, so fakers sometimes paint modern examples then clumsily scrape the paint off, leaving fragments in the crevices. If in doubt, look at the hinges. It is possible they are convincing, but with the connivance of the vendor remove one of the screws. A new screw is easily identifiable. If old screws have been used they will screw out too easily.

History: Early corner cupboards were bow-fronted, sometimes lacquered, sometimes painted, often plain, and were often built-in corner fitments rather than cupboards. Architectural types, with shell-like canopies, were popular in the grand houses for the display of antiquities. Some corner cupboards were made for individual rooms, and they may not be right-angled. Because of the effects of damp, the backs of genuine corner cupboards may have been replaced.

Piece:	**COUNTRY CHAIR**
Material:	Oak
Dimensions:	2ft 10in high, 1ft 6in wide
Period:	*c*.1900
Value:	A

Points to look for: As these are plentiful and bought for use the main criterion is fitness for purpose, though there is variation in the back, with the slats and splats variously disposed or sometimes replaced with spindles. Fruit woods and other country woods command a slight premium over oak. It is virtually impossible to date them, and a similar type of chair was made as a Utility chair from 1943. Unusual proportions or rush seating may indicate that they are nineteenth-century Arts and Crafts chairs and thus considerably more expensive.

History: The kitchen chair, institutional chair, basic household chair, is the triumph of fitness-for-purpose thinking, doing its job perfectly well and fitting into any unpretentious surroundings. It has few elements, and these are all suited to quick production often by makers who had moved from agricultural pursuits to cater for the growing industrial population of the north of England in the nineteenth century. Some country chairs have been given names (ladder-back, Mendlesham), some not. This example is a good one, well proportioned, though perhaps the seat rail is too thin.

Piece:	**COUNTRY SIDE TABLE**
Material:	Fruitwood
Dimensions:	1ft 10in high, 3ft 3in wide
Period:	*c.*1680
Value:	B

Points to look for: Modest, unpretentious, well proportioned, these handy tables, suitable for placing anywhere in the house, are always in demand and often command higher prices than the work involved in making them seems to warrant. There is no question that it is a country piece, and country rather than provincial, where a furniture-maker would probably have made an effort to provide some form of ornamentation, or possibly would have been unable to resist rounding off the corners of the top. The top is unusually thin, a plus rather than minus.

History: Although termed a side table this could have been used almost anywhere, probably in quite a humble capacity. Had there been a tray top it could be provisionally labelled a work table for ladies, especially for bead work which was a fashionable and undemanding hobby (and remained so for nearly two centuries). The style of the turned legs was traditional; the use of the lathe had been known to the humblest craftsmen of the Elizabethan period, and the combination of shapes was easy to obtain with the minimum of effort. Turning became extremely popular when mechanical lathes were invented.

Piece:	**COURT CUPBOARD**
Material:	Oak
Dimensions:	4ft high, 3ft 11in wide
Period:	*c.*1610
Value:	C

POINTS TO LOOK FOR: This is what English furniture was like – bold, confident, and assertive – before Charles II and his ilk introduced fancy Dutch and French ideas. The court cupboard was reproduced throughout the Victorian period and into the 1930s as it proclaimed the essence of old England. How do you tell if it is original? The best way is to get the sniff of it. Does it look right? Is the carving strong and bear the marks of gouges and chisels? Does the wood feel right to touch? Are unseen surfaces such as the back grey and untouched, as they should be? Are the ubiquitous 'melon shapes' convincing?

HISTORY: The word 'court' has nothing to do with royalty but is French for 'short'; the cup-board was orginally a board for cups, by extension a side table for the display of 'cups', which could include plates. The court cupboard was also called a buffet, hall cupboard, or parlour cupboard (the hall was the main room of a house not a mere foyer). Court cupboards can date from the sixteenth century; there are two types, the open and the closed, the latter looking like baleful top-heavy sideboards, but still commanding high prices.

Piece:	**CREDENZA**
Material:	Walnut with marquetry
Dimensions:	4ft high, 5ft wide
Period:	*c*.1860
Value:	C

POINTS TO LOOK FOR: Credenzas are ornate, loaded with veneer or decoration of some kind, any damage involves major repair for almost every surface has been adorned in some way. Although sometimes referred to as side cabinet, the credenza has a personality of its own, often fitted at the ends with glazed display sections, usually with three shelves. It is far too much trouble to fake or make up. The workmanship is often incredible. Crude repairs will show up right away. When checking veneer, go over it very closely, if necessary with a magnifying glass. An intricate all-over design can contain hundreds of pieces.

HISTORY: The credenza evolved, answering the demand of the middle-class Victorians for something flashy which would reflect their taste and aspirations. They wanted value for money and with the credenza they certainly got it, for it may be considered the quintessential piece of classic Victoriana. All woods were used, walnut with marquetry being perhaps the favourite, and credenzas were ebonised, hand painted, adorned with plaques, etc. Some had mirror backs. Marble-topped examples are valued less than wood-topped.

Piece:	**CRICKET TABLE**
Material:	Sycamore
Dimensions:	2ft 2in high, 3ft wide
Period:	Late eighteenth century
Value	B

POINTS TO LOOK FOR: Being a folksy, easily made item of furniture cricket tables may not be what they seem, and the advice with such pieces is to go to a specialist dealer who has a feel for what is the genuine article. Sycamore is not one of the more common woods, but widely used by country makers who often looked around them and saw what trees were around and whether they were suitable for furniture. It is a white wood, similar to plane, fine-grained, taking a high polish, used in marquetry in the seventeenth century, veneer in the late eighteenth. It seems that this particular table has had a batten put on beneath the table top, perhaps to counter incipient or actual warping.

HISTORY: In 1643 the name cricket was given to a low wooden stool. Why the cricket table is so called is something of a mystery. What is certain is that in old paintings of farmhouse interiors the three-legged cricket table occupies a prominent place, the main reason being that for uneven floors three legs are more stable than four. Unquestionably a country piece, widely used, devoid of ornament, oblivious to changing fashions.

Piece:	**DAVENPORT DESK**
Material:	Birds-eye maple
Dimensions:	2ft wide
Period:	*c.*1850
Value:	C

POINTS TO LOOK FOR: The rarer woods, such as burr walnut, satinwood and birds-eye maple are preferred, and secret drawers, galleried tops, complex interior arrangements, clever gadgetry all carry a premium. Cabriole legs are more desirable, and all classic Davenports have four real drawers on one side, four dummy drawers on the other. The example above is top quality, with a rising rear section containing pigeon holes and four drawers. Ornate Victorian Davenports are worth more than plainer earlier ones. Davenports without a base, just a desk top on legs, are not highly regarded (only relatively speaking).

HISTORY: In the 1790s a Captain Davenport ordered from the firm of Gillow's a desk of a specific kind. It proved immediately popular. They were 'very useful articles for industrious young ladies' wrote J.C. Loudon in his *Encyclopaedia of Cottage, Farm and Villa Architecture* (1833). Early examples are no more than small chests of drawers with sliding desk compartments on top (to accommodate the knees). Later versions, there are at least forty-five of them, could be endlessly extravagant and marvellous.

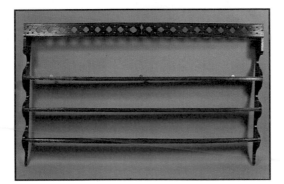

Piece:	**DELFT RACK**
Material:	Oak
Dimensions:	3ft 10in high, 4ft 8in wide
Period:	*c.*1770
Value:	B

POINTS TO LOOK FOR: It may be that the Delft racks are on the borderline of antique furniture, and earn entrance simply because a certain amount of show goes into them. Because of their simplicity, it follows that a period Delft rack is an easy target for fakers, with the shelves made from old floor boards and the fretted frieze made from a handy section of period oak. The frieze cut-outs are the most likely to give a clue to whether a piece is genuine, as of course they would have been painstakingly cut out by hand without any mechanical aids, and the marks of a modern jigsaw are unmistakeable.

HISTORY: The eighteenth century was the first age when the well-to-do were joined by the middle classes in the collecting of antiques. Antiques means items from antiquity, which in turn meant to the acquiring classes the world of ancient Greece and Rome, but the scope was being broadened, and amongst the new collectables was the blue-and-white tin-glazed pottery of Delft in the Netherlands, made to imitate Chinese porcelain. By the time this rack was made true porcelain was manufactured in Europe, and the rack would have been used for any pretty ceramic pieces, Delft or not.

Piece:	**DEMI-LUNE SIDEBOARD**
Materials:	Satinwood and marquetry
Dimensions:	3ft high, 4ft 10in wide
Period:	Nineteenth century
Value:	E

POINTS TO LOOK FOR: At first glance, or even a second, this might appear to be a genuine period piece, and the price it achieved at auction (£5200) seems to bear this out. Why, then, have the auctioneers, a highly respected house in the south-west, classified it ambiguously as merely nineteenth century? Perhaps it may be too fiddly to be Georgian or Regency. The elipsoid inlay sections into which the handles are set are perhaps ungainly, the decoration running down the legs too trivial, and the handles seem to have the 'stamped-out' look of mass production. The marquetry top would certainly not bear the wear and tear of a working sideboard.

HISTORY: The sideboard, a necessary adjunct to elegant eating in the eighteenth century, was capable of many variations, the demi-lune (half-moon) shape was not one of the better options, with little working space for the servants one of the characteristics of bow-front furniture is that things tend to fall off it. The classic sideboard had cupboards used to store wine, and this would be a difficult feat in a sideboard such as this. Nevertheless, as a display piece, the demi-lune sideboard has a niche.

Piece:	**D-END TWIN-PEDESTAL DINING TABLE**
Material:	Mahogany.
Dimensions:	9ft wide, 3ft 11in deep.
Period:	*c.*1800
Value:	E

POINTS TO LOOK FOR: The larger the table the better because these antiques are bought for use rather than show, and for a really massive table with more than two pedestal bases there is no upper price limit. Because such tables have had heavy usage there has been great pressure on the pedestals, and their tripod legs are quite vulnerable as they are slotted into the upright. If there is damage it is likely to be here. Some surface staining is acceptable. French polishing reduces the table's value. Scuffing on the legs due to diners' feet is not detrimental; a good waxing will remedy this.

HISTORY: The pedestal table was introduced as an answer to the problem of 'legs under the table' in the late eighteenth-century when eating was a fine art and large dinner parties were popular. Many pedestal dining tables could be fitted out with extra leaves (make certain that they match), and some of the methods for sliding in these extra leaves were very ingenious and were sometimes patented. A patent table is extra desirable. Some dining tables were fitted with flaps, so that the length could be reduced. As a piece of useful furniture it has never been improved upon.

Piece:	**DRESSER**
Material:	Oak
Dimensions:	2ft 10in high, 5ft 10in wide.
Period:	*c.*1730
Value:	C

POINTS TO LOOK FOR: Dressers come in all shapes and sizes, mostly oak and pine, some with a superstructure, some without. The most suspect are pine dressers, at the foot of the value scale, sometimes made up from odds and ends of wood. Pine dressers can be stripped with caustic soda, softening the wood and loosening the joints. An oak dresser base reputed to be self-sufficient should be examined on the top to see if it ever had a superstructure – look for recent signs of renovation and tarting up, and also for any unexplained screwholes. Check that the handles look right.

HISTORY: The dresser derives from side tables and boards. Food was 'dressed' on the dresser, thus the name. Early oak dressers from about 1650 are long and low with several drawers, but from about 1700 a superstructure of shelves and/or cupboards began to be used. The dresser is frequently associated with Wales, which had its own speciality, the tridarn. The pine dresser was often Welsh, with open shelves until 1840 when some glazing was introduced, with total glazing from about 1870. Few pine dressers can be said with certainty to be earlier than 1800. Plywood was used from the 1890s.

Piece:	**D-SHAPED FOLDING CARD TABLE**
Material:	Satinwood with amboyna banding
Dimensions:	3ft wide
Period:	*c.*1785
Value:	C

POINTS TO LOOK FOR: Make certain this type of table does fold over properly, and the top has not become distorted. Folded tables are usually placed against a wall, and if there are central-heating radiators they can cause havoc to the wood. Check the hinges, tightening screws. The condition of the baize (revealed when the top is open) is of minor importance; it can easily be replaced. Legs are often slender and tapered, so look for signs of stress. Examine the feet. Spade feet can chip off with the grain.

HISTORY: The card table, logically enough, arose from the eighteenth-century passion for cards. In 1728 whist became immensely fashionable, written about by Hoyle in the 1730s, and it remained so until replaced by bridge. The card table when not in use was kept folded by the wall, pulled out into the room when needed. It could also be a rectangular table, folding out into a square, often with a swivel top, sometimes of rosewood, calamander, burr elm, and other exotic woods, and ornately carved, especially in the Victorian period. Some card tables have recesses for counters and facilities for candleholders.

Piece:	**DWARF BREAKFRONT BOOKCASE**
Material:	Mahogany and brass
Dimensions:	3ft 2in high, 5 ft long
Period:	*c.*1810
Value:	C

POINTS TO LOOK FOR: This is as much a display piece as a bookcase, and paying a price like this means the owner is not so concerned with cramming as many books in as possible. However, when buying a cheaper dwarf bookcase for use make certain it is sensible, that the shelves are not set too close together so that they are useless except for paperbacks, and that the shelves are deep enough. Dwarf unglazed bookcases are ideal in that every inch is exposed and there are no hidden perils. The intricate brass inlay should be closely examined to see it is not lifting, though it is simple to put right by nipping off a fraction and resetting. And is the marble top original?

HISTORY: Low-level furniture, solid and uncompromising with assertive surface decoration, was extremely popular in the early years of the nineteenth century throughout Europe and America. Interiors lost the formal grace of the eighteenth century, and were more variously and innovatively furnished. Some dwarf bookcases were movable and made to house books on both sides, about the period of this bookcase the revolving bookcase was introduced.

Piece:	**EDWARDIAN DISPLAY CABINET**
Material:	Mahogany
Dimensions:	3ft 1in high, 1ft 6in wide
Period:	*c.*1905
Value:	A

POINTS TO LOOK FOR: There is no danger confusing an Edwardian piece with an eighteenth-century article as this type of article was not made in the Georgian period. Characteristic are the spade feet and the stringing of satinwood, the quality of the woodwork cannot be faulted, though the brass fittings are often inferior and often have echoes of the Art Nouveau style which co-existed in the early years of the twentieth century. A type of furniture undervalued and still within reach by those on a modest budget, but the condition must be good.

HISTORY: The display cabinet is not a classic piece, though collectors in the early nineteenth century had glazed cabinets to show their treasures, and it has achieved its apotheosis in the Victorian period with the ebonised giants often called vitrines. The smaller more sedate Edwardian display pieces reflect a considered rejection of Victorian clutter in favour of a more refined presentation. The 1920s and 1930s once again enlivened the display cabinet with silvered and frosted glass, trendy motifs such as the sun ray, and all the trimmings.

Piece:	**ENCOIGNURE**
Material:	Ebonised wood and boulle
Dimensions:	3ft 8in high, 2ft 4in wide
Period:	*c.*1860
Value:	B

POINTS TO LOOK FOR: The tortoise-shell and brass inlay (boulle) should be in good condition, and try to ascertain that it is original and not 1920s and 1930s imitation tortoiseshell added later (natural tortoiseshell has a grain). This cabinet is bow fronted. Ebonising is done on close-grained wood such as pear. In English furniture ebonised wood is not liked, but this is a French piece and acceptable. Any surface scuffing where the base wood shows through can be remedied by the application of shoe polish.

HISTORY: The display cabinet is an elusive creature, merging into the side cabinet, the music cabinet, the bookcase, and the vitrine. If it is continental, it also has a variety of names, such as, in this case, the encoignure. This example is known to be French rather than British because of the confident use of boulle. Towards the end of the nineteenth century display cabinets could be intricate and adventurous in all the fashionable Aesthetic and Art Nouveau styles, and in the 1920s and 1930s it became an essential parlour piece with 'sun ray' motifs and silvering on the glass.

Piece:	**FOLDING CARD TABLE**
Material:	Thuyawood and marquetry
Dimensions:	3ft 3in wide
Period:	*c.*1870
Value:	B

Points to look for: This card table was made in France, and there are several features which distinguish it from its British equivalent. The thuya or thuja tree is a kind of a juniper, not greatly used in British furniture at this time, and in Britain ebonising was often unconvincing, regarded as a second-best. Here it is the ground for quite breathtaking floral inlay work on the top. The legs have a studied elegance with just enough decoration to set off the marquetry above them. The gilt-metal mounts would also have been less confident if applied to a British table of the period.

History: Card playing was quite as popular in France as in Britain, and a great variety of tables were introduced, many of them folding and secreted away until they were needed. Throughout the nineteenth century, revivalist styles were common throughout Europe. In Britain it was called the Gothic, in Italy the Dantesque, and in France the Troubadour, but this piece, though echoing eighteenth-century elegance, is definitely of its period. The high quality is exemplified by the distinctive touches, such as the fact that the table when opened is not quite square but has graceful moulded edges.

Piece:	**FRAMED TABLE**
Material:	Mahogany
Dimensions:	8ft long
Period:	*c.*1850
Value:	C

POINTS TO LOOK FOR: This is technically a library table because it has a leather top and drawers, and the term framed table denotes its construction (a leg in each corner). The period when it was made is indicated by the shape and decoration of the legs. Frame tables come in all woods and in all sizes. At the bottom of the range is the kitchen table, at the top the refectory table. Large 'family' tables are usually plain on top. Scratches, indentations, even chips, are no problem to a restorer, providing the top is solid.

HISTORY: Framed tables have been made throughout the history of furniture. There is an Egyptian table in existence dating from about 1600BC which could have been made yesterday. The 'modern' framed table with fixed tops and heavy turned legs was introduced in the sixteenth century when private rooms, rather than a multi-purpose room for eating, sleeping and all-round roistering, became the norm. Among the many examples is the draw-leaf table; Victorian wind-up ones were widely neglected, but are now becoming quite valuable. These often lie neglected in garages and workshops. The framed method could also be used for circular fixed-top tables.

Piece:	**GALLERIED SIDEBOARD**
Material:	Mahogany with crossbanding
Dimensions:	3ft 2in high, 6ft 2in wide
Period:	*c.*1790
Value:	D

Points to look for: This is a thoroughbred of a sideboard and there is no danger of it being mistaken for a dressing table or anything else. The cupboards at the side for cooling or storing wine are splendidly presented. There are actually two drawers; the arched apron is the second, below the cutlery drawer. As usual, there are six legs, each of which should be examined for weakness, but the most vulnerable part is the crossbanding, wood cut across the grain. Any damage or stress to the carcase of the sideboard can cause tiny oblongs of crossbanding to flip out. This is easy to repair. If substitute crossbanding does not match it can be stained.

History: 1790, about which time this sideboard was made, was a period when history was moving fast, and the first elements of what became the Regency period are appearing, best represented by the stark brass gallery, the austerity redeemed by the delicate modelling of the uprights. The tapering square-section legs are perfectly plain. There was no need for any decoration. It may be that such a piece as this represents the very best of English furniture, and the future fashion for replacing the legs with cupboards was an unmitigated disaster.

Piece:	**GAMES TABLE**
Material:	Mahogany
Dimensions:	2ft 5in high, 2ft 5in wide
	(with flaps up)
Period:	*c.*1815
Value:	C

Points to look for: All should be complete, for many games tables contain extras. The chess board should be contemporary with the table, and not replaced because of wear on the original. The squares are usually inlay of ebony and boxwood, and there is a tendency for them to lift after a century and a half of usage. The backgammon surface, hidden when the flaps draw together, is usually less prone to wear. End supports are more desirable than a central pedestal with tripod or quadripod legs. This is a superior example. Lesser pieces sometimes have dummy drawers. The object on top of this games table has nothing to do with the piece; it is an eighteenth-century tea caddy made from rolled paper.

History: Civilized societies demand civilized games. Chess was long established, but blossomed in the eighteenth century when a properly organized chess club was formed at a coffee house in St Martin's Lane, London. Backgammon was known in Britain from at least the tenth century. Cards, of course, were far more popular. Some games tables had bags beneath, often of pleated silk, or, by about 1870, a funnel. There is a narrow dividing line between games tables and work tables.

Piece:	**GATELEG TABLE**
Material:	Oak
Dimensions:	1ft 10in high, 2ft 2in wide
Period:	*c.*1690
Value:	B

POINTS TO LOOK FOR: Make certain that the gate actually works, and that when extended the table-top runs flush and there is no warping. The extending leaves should be closely compared with the fixed section to see that they match. Buckled hinges on the underside will mean that some time in the past something has gone wrong. If the oak planks that are used in the top are too narrow it might mean a made-up piece, though there is no hard or fast rule as such tables were made for modest country folk as well as for the grand. As with all hard-working furniture, signs of usage are welcome, especially on the stretchers where diners' feet rested.

HISTORY: Gateleg tables exist from the early seventeenth century, but it was only in the 1650s that they came into general use, coinciding with greater informality and the use of smaller rooms to dine in. Some of the gateleg mechanisms could be very elaborate. The gateleg shown is about the simplest, quite adequate for a four seater. Although ingenious, the structure of the table got in the way of the legs, as it did in the Georgian D-end table. The problem was solved with the multi-pedestal table (from about 1780).

Piece:	**GENTLEMAN'S PRESS**
Material:	Ash
Dimensions:	6ft 6in high, 3ft 7in wide
Period:	*c*.1790
Value:	B

Points to look for: This particular example of a press is possibly entitled a gentleman's press because of its angularity and lack of obtrusive ornament. Its main feature is the ebony surrounds to the doors, and the fact that it is made of ash. Ash is a greyish-white wood with light brown veining, is subject to woodworm, and after 1700 was largely used for cheap country furniture. In late Georgian times ash was prized because of the delicacy of its figuration, as seen in the doors of this piece. A no-nonsense article where anything wrong can be seen immediately.

History: The word press is one of those which has a multitude of meanings, and many people find it a puzzling name for a piece of furniture which closely resembles a wardrobe, and indeed is a wardrobe until the top doors are opened disclosing banks of drawers not hanging rails, or even a folding bed (the press bed). Drawers were used instead of rails as it was the custom to fold clothes rather than hang them. As presses were bedroom furniture they were usually plain, and despite the often superb workmanship they remain non-display pieces, bought for use rather than show.

Piece:	**GEORGIAN WORK TABLE.**
Material:	Rosewood
Dimensions:	2ft 4in high, 1ft 7 in wide
Period:	Late eighteenth-century.
Value:	C

Points to look for: Work tables were made in a variety of shapes and styles, many with a bag or funnel beneath to hold the contents. The eighteenth-century examples are the easiest to assess, as they are mostly straight forward, in this case with a drawer and not a lift-up top. Any banding, stringing or inlay should be closely examined for signs of repair or replacement, or later 'improvement.' Long slender legs are vulnerable, and should be checked for repair or weakness. Castors should be in keeping, preferably fitted on with caps not screwed in. Original fittings and interior fabrics are a major plus.

History: Work tables appeared in the eighteenth-century, and should really be called play or hobby tables as they were repositories for needlework and embroidery implements and items associated with games such as chess and backgammon. Some work tables had fold-over tops which, when opened, revealed backgammon and chess boards. Chippendale did not illustrate any, but Sheraton, noted for his ingenuity, designed a variety of them. In the Victorian period work tables were often ornate prestige pieces for women in top woods, and these are greatly in demand.

Piece:	**GORDON RUSSELL WARDROBE**
Material:	Walnut
Dimensions:	6ft 8in high, 7ft wide
Period:	1928
Value:	B

POINTS TO LOOK FOR: In furniture of the 1920s and 1930s quality is all, and unlike antique furniture before, say, 1830 condition is of vital importance, scratches and bruises are inadmissible. This means that any damage will have been as cleverly repaired as is humanly possible. Quality furniture by major manufacturers was often labelled, and this label makes a massive difference in the price. False labels may be applied. A label may not be immediately obvious; on sideboards they may be inside the drawers. Sometimes it is not easy to differentiate between designer and chain-store furniture.

HISTORY: The wardrobe derived from the clothes press, the main difference being the provision of facilities for hanging clothes. During the nineteenth century, and with the enthusiasm for clothing accessories, drawers were often incorporated. Gordon Russell (1892–1980) was arguably the most important English furniture designer of the twentieth century. Initially based at Broadway, Worcestershire, he was a follower of the famous furniture designer Ernest Gimson (1864–1919). Gimson's workshops made an almost identical wardrobe to this.

Piece:	**GOTHICK CHAIR**
Material:	Oak
Dimensions:	4ft high, 1ft 10 in wide
Period:	*c.*1750
Value:	C

POINTS TO LOOK FOR: The spelling Gothick is an indication that the piece belongs to the Gothic Revival and is not medieval, and there should be no difficulty in differentiating the two, nor in establishing the difference between furniture of the eighteenth and nineteenth centuries. Eighteenth-century Gothick furniture was elegant, well in tune with the period, and the two chairs illustrated are as splendidly carved as anything in the Chippendale canon, even though they are in oak. Look for cunning alterations, such as added mouldings, to turn a piece of nondescript furniture into something out of the ordinary.

HISTORY: The revival of Gothic styles was a gentlemanly hobby from about 1740, the key figure being Horace Walpole (1717–1797), writer and connoisseur. Gothic was a term used in objurgation, and only became respectable when taken up by the Romantic writers. Gothick was a dainty reworking of old themes, and only with the arrival of Pugin (1812–52) was there any serious attempt to be historically accurate, attempts that were mostly ignored in the manufacturers' desire to pile detail on detail until any structure was all but hidden.

Piece:	**GOTHIC-STYLE DISPLAY CABINET**
Material:	*Pine*
Dimensions:	5ft 8in high, 3ft wide
Period:	1991
Value:	A

POINTS TO LOOK FOR: If this were not so obviously fresh from the workshops and had been subjected to the distressing process to make it look old, it might be difficult to date this piece, which was made to special order. The Gothic style was not often used in pine; oak was far more suited, as pine is less crisp for the carver's tools – and carving is the essence of Gothic. In this piece there are no end of anachronisms, but this was also true of nineteenth-century Gothic.

HISTORY: Since it became fashionable in the early nineteenth century, the Gothic style has never really died, and still makes an occasional appearance. The Gothic style was never remotely like the real Gothic (*c*1140–*c*.1560), and was concerned with prettified ecclesiastical motifs such as arches, spires, and uncomfortable angularity. It made an appearance in American clocks, Victorian architecture, and in flamboyant Victorian furniture, often looking like stone rather than wood, sometimes using rosewood, bird's-eye maple and satinwood against oak. Sometimes the oak was oiled, not stained, giving a curious orange colour. Fakers, take note.

Piece:	**HANGING CORNER CUPBOARD**
Material:	Walnut
Dimensions:	3ft 3in high, 2ft wide
Period:	*c.*1720
Value:	B

POINTS TO LOOK FOR: Corner cupboards, especially the hanging type, were very vulnerable to damp, and there is a likelihood that at some time the back has been replaced. This does not detract too greatly. This bow-fronted example is a classic type, produced almost unaltered throughout the eighteenth century except that walnut gave way to mahogany. Some corner cupboards had pediments, often added much later, and where there is busy inlay it is possible that this may be an Edwardian addition. A curious feature of some hanging cupboards is that the interiors have been painted orange or blue. Glazed corner cupboards are very popular, so much so that solid-fronted examples have been quietly converted.

HISTORY: The hanging cupboard was never so popular with the wealthy as a display piece for their china and little treasures as the free-standing type, perhaps because there was always a chance of it falling off the wall and damaging their china (which was always valued more highly than mere furniture). The Victorians did not care for it, though it enjoyed a revival in the 1920s. Some hanging cupboards had drawers, making them more desirable.

Piece:	**HEPPLEWHITE CHAIR**
Material:	Mahogany
Dimensions:	3ft high, 2ft 8in wide
Period:	*c.*1790
Value:	E for set of eight

POINTS TO LOOK FOR: 'Long' sets of chairs (six or more) are much desired. A pair of chairs is worth around three times the single chair price, a set of four six to seven times the single chair price, a set of six ten to twelve times the single chair price, and a set of eight fifteen times the single chair price. It is not uncommon for vendors of long sets to 'spread the damage around' to make the chairs look respectable if not perfect. This particular set consists of six ordinary chairs plus two armchairs or carvers. The seats are of hide, and the method of upholstery is superior to drop-in types.

HISTORY: George Hepplewhite died in 1786. His influential *The Cabinet-maker and Upholsterer's Guide* was published posthumously in 1788. In his time he was not regarded highly, but he epitomises Georgian elegance, making camel-back, hoop-back and serpentine-fronted chairs, though perhaps best known for the shield-back design and his use of the Prince of Wales feathers motif. He favoured tapered fluted legs and leaf and swag carving. English chair design in the eighteenth century was the most progressive in Europe, due to makers and designers such as Chippendale, Sheraton, and Hepplewhite.

Piece:	**ITALIAN JEWEL CABINET ON STAND**
Material:	Walnut and gilt metal
Dimensions:	6ft high, 4ft 6in wide
Period:	Seventeenth century
Value:	D

POINTS TO LOOK FOR: This Italian cabinet is so different from English furniture that it involves a totally new way of looking at it, with little to compare it with it may even be difficult to slot the piece into its correct century. It is certainly more cosmopolitan than any British furniture of the time. The description as a jewel cabinet is speculative. There is such a profusion of added ornament that it all needs to be examined. Unlike many English cabinets on stands the legs are sturdy without design weaknesses, so it is likely to be original, especially as the style of decoration of the stand is in keeping.

HISTORY: It was early realised in France and Italy that the top of the basic receptacle, the chest, could be used as a seat or table, suggesting a front opening instead of the top, the first stage in the evolution of the cabinet. Putting the cabinet on legs made it easier to see into the drawers or cupboards. In the early seventeenth century the cabinet was the dominant article of European furniture, embellished by carving, marquetry, inlay of precious stones, often with gilt-metal mounts.

Piece:	**KNEEHOLE DESK**
Materials:	Mahogany
Dimensions:	2ft 5in high, 2ft 11in wide
Period:	*c.*1740
Value:	C

POINTS TO LOOK FOR: The great advantage of a kneehole desk is that it can be taken apart for a close inspection as it is merely banks of drawers and a cupboard. Handles should preferably be contemporary (these are), but if not should be in keeping and, above all, matching. If replacement handles are sought it is vital that the key escutcheons, both on the drawer and on the cupboard, should be appropriate. An interesting point is that the H-shape hinges of the cupboard are on the outside. A good guide to dating is the type of bracket feet; had the desk been later than George II they would have been shaped more.

HISTORY: This is most likely not a kneehole desk but a dressing table, and the naming of antique furniture is often arbitrary, determined by the needs of a buyer. It is possibly more suitable as a desk. With the kneehole dressing table the long top drawer was fitted with boxes, compartments, and a hinged toilet mirror. That they were intended for occasional writing is affirmed by the occasional presence of a baize-covered top. Sometimes the top itself is hinged. The kneehole dressing table was made in walnut early in the century.

Piece:	**LADIES' WRITING TABLE**
Material:	Rosewood
Dimensions:	2ft 5in high, 2ft 8in wide
Period:	*c*.1820
Value:	C

POINTS TO LOOK FOR: Elegance being the watchword of the time so far as ladies were concerned, anything which detracts from it is suspect, and may indicate a conversion from a humbler piece such as a single-drawer side table. There could be a good deal of variation. In this very superior piece the top is edged top and bottom with brass, not usual, and the rising fire screen is a charming extra. The turned legs are restrained, denoting a date in the early nineteenth century. The original leather top is a plus, but a buyer would have to weigh up the claims of a clean replacement over perhaps an ink-stained original.

HISTORY: Men's and women's writing tables pursued different directions. Men's tables were increasingly robust and manly with a large surface area, characteristic of which was the double pedestal type. Women's tables were often far too cute, frequently fragile, and the writing surfaces were often miniscule, perhaps all right for diary entries and messages to the cook. The reason for the popularity of the screen is interesting; coal was now used in towns and cities instead of wood. It gave out far more heat and delicate complexions needed to be protected.

Piece:	**LIBRARY CHAIR**
Material:	Walnut
Dimensions:	3ft high, 2ft wide
Period:	*c.*1725
Value:	B

POINTS TO LOOK FOR: These are sometimes described as corner chairs, and are evaluated exactly the same as an ordinary chair, checking for any kind of repairs to the legs or the splats, especially necessary when these are refined or perforated as in eighteenth-century mahogany chairs. Perhaps the most vulnerable parts of this sturdy no-nonsense chair are the ball-and-claw feet which, as they protrude, might tend to become bruised, or the knees of the cabriole leg. The stout back is further supported by turned pillars, which would preclude sitting astride facing-the-back, a facility of many such chairs.

HISTORY: The writing chair was a sensible development of the workaday chair, and it is surprising that it has fallen from fashion because the fact that the user sits above a single front leg means that the arms of the chair do not interfere with the ability to write. It is also helpful because the chair can be pulled in closer to a writing surface. This type of chair was transitional, and although squat anticipated the elegance of the mahogany chairs which were to render walnut obsolete in a few years time.

Piece:	**LIBRARY STEPS**
Material:	Mahogany and cane
Dimensions:	4ft 6in high
Period:	*c.*1820
Value:	B

Points to look for: Check that the hinges that turn the chair into a pair of steps are in order. If the legs are reeded, and curved as well, ascertain that they are in good repair as it is expensive to repair or replace them. If the terminals to the arms are curved round they are vulnerable, as they may snap off with the grain. Dirt is inclined to get into the grooves of the reeding and build up into a hard body, needing strenuous efforts to probe out. Caned seats are expensive to replace. For weaknesses, examine where the cane is attached to the wood.

History: It was not until the late seventeenth century that books were put into bookcases, but in the eighteenth century bookcases became huge. Reaching the upper shelves was difficult without aids, ranging from a step ladder to ingenious combination furniture. Some were simple; a stool tips on end to become two steep steps; armchairs divide into halves; a hinged table top has steps on the underside and pulls out to rest at an angle of forty-five degrees on the edge of the table while inside the table is another flight of steps arranged to form a continuation, altogether about eight feet in length.

Piece:	**LIBRARY TABLE**
Material:	Rosewood with gilt-metal mounts
Dimensions:	4ft 9in long
Period:	*c.*1820
Value:	D

POINTS TO LOOK FOR: Library tables were made for use rather than ornament, and were often very sturdy. An odd feature was that some of them were equipped not only with real drawers but dummy drawers as well, and a hard tug on the knob or handle of a drawer that seems to be sticking could result in embarrassment. Although library tables were long writing tables, they could also be used as general purpose drawing-room furniture, so the top should be studied for stains of all kinds, not just the ink stains (easy to remove) expected on a library table.

HISTORY: Library tables of massive form, with pedestal bases, appeared in the early-eighteenth century, often richly carved, with gilt-metal mounts. This style did not persist after about 1740. Plainer types appeared, with end supports with four small feet being perhaps the most common. Oval, round, and kidney-shaped (so termed 'on account of its resemblance to that intestine part of animals') library tables were also made. During the Regency period lyre-ended tables were popular. The Victorians favoured inlaid tops and also bobbin turning on the legs and stretchers (not so valuable).

Piece:	**LIVERY CUPBOARD**
Material:	Oak
Dimensions:	3ft 6in high, 5ft 2in wide
Period:	*c.*1525
Value:	D

POINTS TO LOOK FOR: For a piece of this age damage, sometimes severe damage, is of less importance than wood colour and genuineness. The damaged and missing key escutcheons are of little consequence. More important is the convincing petalled Gothic roundel in the cupboard doors and the formalised near-linen-fold carving. The stubby and much worn feet have been left as they are after nearly five centuries on mostly stone floors. Furniture like this is notoriously difficult to date, or even to assign to a particular country though this piece is most likely to be English.

HISTORY: At this time furniture made by English craftsmen was often inferior to that made by the French, the Germans, and especially the Italians, who began to have an effect on English design from about 1530, though a guild of carpenters had been in existence in Britain since the early fourteenth century. The livery cupboard was a food cupboard; the food was delivered (livrée) from these cupboards, also known as aumbries or dole cupboards. Names given to late medieval pieces are usually speculative. This may not be a livery cupboard as there is no means of ventilation, no open tracery.

Piece:	**LOWBOY**
Material:	Oak and walnut
Dimensions:	2ft 3in high, 2ft 9in wide
Period:	*c*.1720
Value:	C

POINTS TO LOOK FOR: This is George I period when walnut was still the principle wood for making furniture, and when oak was still used. Elegance is not expected, though this piece has it, not only in the delicately shaped apron but in the assured cabriole legs with pad feet. One would expect some wear, and pad feet, due to the run of the grain, could be vulnerable, so check that there is no undue damage, though bruising is acceptable. With five handles to examine there is always the chance that one might be a 'foreigner', ie a replacement. The top should be well-used, perhaps ingrained with long-applied wax.

HISTORY: There is learned debate whether such an article of furniture should be called a side table or a lowboy, but current opinion is that if there are more than two drawers it should be termed a lowboy, a term not to be found in the *Shorter Oxford English Dictionary* for some obscure no doubt pedantic reason. Side tables and lowboys were used when society became more informal and occasional tables were placed casually around the rooms. The chunky and compact lowboy was far more suited to walnut than mahogany.

Piece:	**LYRE-BACK DINING CHAIR**
Material:	Mahogany
Dimensions:	3ft high, 1ft 6in wide
Period:	*c.*1815
Value:	E set of eight

POINTS TO LOOK FOR: The quality of the carving of the lyre-shaped splat should be crisp and clean. The wood is of quite thick section and is thus less likely to have had a break. Where the wood is thin, a break may have been cosmetically treated, relying on the slat to support the weight of the diner's back. The uprights are grooved, and after nearly two hundred years these grooves tend to build up with polish. However, this set is of the highest quality and superbly presented. The sabre leg is always vulnerable because of the direction of the grain.

HISTORY: Dining chairs, more solid and roomy than 'casual' chairs though sharing their design characteristics, came to prominence when eating habits became formalised and it was no longer necessary for a guest to bring his or her own cutlery. A set included two carvers for the host and his wife, the same shaped chair with arms. The lyre motif, Greek rather than Roman, was introduced during the neo-Classical phase in the eighteenth century and was particularly popular in America, being a favourite of the most important American cabinet-maker Duncan Phyfe.

Piece:	**MARBLE-TOP CENTRE TABLE**
Material:	Rosewood
Dimenions:	3ft high, 2ft 4in wide
Period:	*c*.1815
Value:	E

Points to look for: This table is perfectly of its period with its acanthus decoration and the use of parcel gilding (part gilding) and the inimitable scroll feet. Tables of this type with a central pillar and a sturdy platform base are free from hidden stresses though with the weight of the marble top it is wise to look underneath to see what is happening there and if the structure holding the top is secure. Unlike some materials used in mosaic, marble does not suffer from age. White marble should be cleaned with soap and water, coloured marble with petrol.

History: The use of inlays of marble and precious and semi-precious stones was rarer in Britain than it was in Europe, but during the 'show' years of the early nineteenth century the possibilities of creating gorgeous furniture and architecture – Marble Arch dates from 1830 – without being vulgar were fully explored. Later the Victorians, who adored marble, took vulgarity on board. Marble was largely imported from Italy, and became cheap (£4 a ton about 1880). The occasional table, often round, was ideal to show off what were known as specimen marbles.

Piece:	**MARQUETRY CABINET.**
Material:	Various woods with marble top
Dimensions:	4ft 6in high, 4ft 6in wide
Period:	Nineteenth century.
Value:	C

POINTS TO LOOK FOR: This is one of those busy pieces of furniture, well made, and certainly continental. The metal fittings are decidedly un-English. The type of furniture very popular with the new rich because there is a lot going on and high-class marquetry always arouses awe. Dating such furniture is incredibly difficult. The shape of the legs is elegant, but the curious claw feet are incredibly ugly. Because of the work involved, no-one fakes this kind of furniture. Look for missing pieces of marquetry and sections which don't make sense. (Look at the flag-shaped section on the door. What does this mean?)

HISTORY: Of all the types of furniture, the cabinet, which goes under a number of names, has the most variations, not only on the outside but on the inside as well. There may be cupboards, drawers, pigeon-holes, almost anything. Developed in the eighteenth century it reached its apotheosis in the nineteenth, with every conceivable wood and finish, including boulle (tortoise-shell and brass), inset porcelain and pottery plaques, brass grille work, inlaid mosaic, and of course marquetry.

Piece:	**MINIATURE BUREAU BOOKCASE**
Material:	Oak
Dimensions:	4ft high, 2ft 8in wide
Period:	*c*.1780
Value	D

POINTS TO LOOK FOR: It might be thought unusual for oak to be employed for a bureau bookcase as late as the 1780s, but in the country the London fashion for mahogany was considered excessive. However, even if this piece were to be mahogany it would be easy to discern its out-of-town origins by the curious lack of proportion of the swan-neck pediment and the tiny urns. The bookcase section is squat, not much more than half the height of the bureau. The handles are a curious hybrid. However, part of the ineffable charm of miniature furniture is in its inevitable departure from standard norms.

HISTORY: Miniature furniture has always had a great appeal for women, and small chests of drawers are more sought after than 'standard' sizes. The lower storage capacity is of no importance. Country furniture, apart from chairs, is ill documented, and no-one can say whether this was a specific commission or a furniture-maker's fantasy. At one time undersized furniture was automatically classified as apprentice pieces. It would be idle to claim that the bureau bookcase itself was enormously useful; the miniature would be hardly less so.

Piece:	**MINIATURE CHESTS OF DRAWERS**
Materials:	Mahogany and walnut
Dimensions:	1ft 6in high, 2ft wide
Period:	Nineteenth century
Value:	A

POINTS TO LOOK FOR: Collectors of miniature furniture are perfectionists and defects which would be overlooked in a full-size piece are not permitted – such as the broken leg in the mahogany example on the left. The standard procedures for full-sized furniture should be followed – the furniture should look right, the fittings should not be anachronistic, any carving should be crisp, drawers should open easily and not slop about, and the patina and colouring of the wood should be acceptable.

HISTORY: There are a number of theories revolving around miniature furniture and all of them may be right to some degree or other. Were these apprentice pieces, executed to the acclaim of senior master craftsmen? They are too big for doll's house furniture, but this does not exclude the possibility that they were made for children for use in whatever Wendy houses were called at the time. Were they produced by amateur cabinet-makers to demonstrate their skills, or, perhaps one of the favourite theories, were they samples for furniture-makers' representatives to take around with them? All have their supporters.

Piece:	**MULE CHEST**
Material:	Oak and inlay
Dimensions:	3ft 3in high, 4ft 8in wide
Period:	Elizabethan
Value:	B

POINTS TO LOOK FOR: Many of such objects are often described as 'reconstructed', as this one is. Reconstruction can mean anything. The front is very busy, and to decide what is genuine and what is not is a major task. The diamond shapes above the plinth could have been put in any time. The knobs on the drawers look distinctly odd. The twin panels may be authentic, but they would need very close scrutiny. Furniture from this period can look strange; inlaying oak was often a hit or miss process, and many feel that oak should be left as it is – honest, uncompromising, and easier to assess.

HISTORY: The chest was the most important object in the medieval household, used for storage, as a seat, and as a surface for putting things on. It remained so for centuries. The simplest chests were plank coffers, boards nailed onto slab ends. The sides could extend beyond the body of the chest and serve as legs. Ornamentation was often linenfold, wood carved to imitate folded cloth, which gave way to more adventurous carving. Chests made for valuables had complex locks, sometimes three in number. Inlay succeeded carving, and drawers were fitted, leading to the evolution of the chest of drawers.

Piece:	**OCCASIONAL TABLE**
Materials:	Mahogany
Dimensions:	2ft 6in high, 2ft wide
Period:	c. 1910
Value:	A

Points to look for: A low-value piece further reduced in desirability by the removal of a brass name plate on the lower stage, though the screw holes could easily be filled in by the use of a filler and the surface waxed and polished, or even French polished. French polish should never be used on eighteenth-century furniture, but there can be no objection when it comes to run-of-the-mill Edwardian furniture. The underside of the top and the lower stage should be examined to make certain that the legs are adequately set in.

History: The occasional round table has gone through a large number of permutations and has been used for a variety of purposes, as card tables, display tables, and as informal dining tables. Its great disadvantage, unlike the gateleg, is that it cannot be reduced in size and quietly tucked against the wall. The method of fixing the legs (the framed method) and the supporting stretchers to the lower stage means that it is almost indestructible, and consequently there are large numbers about at very little cost. The 1920s and 1930s saw the height of such tables reduced, and these were specified as tea and coffee tables.

Piece:	**OCTAGONAL WINE COOLER**
Materials:	Mahogany with brass
Dimensions:	2ft 3in high, 1ft 9in wide
Period:	*c.*1790
Value:	B

Points to look for: Because of their desirability as decorative drawing-room pieces, wine coolers achieve high prices. Invariably they were splendidly made as only the rich bothered with chilled wine. Efforts to reproduce them have usually foundered not on the woodwork but on the attempt to make the brass encircling the cooler convincing, either by lacquering or by toning it down in some way. The carrying handles were often lion's-mask types. Wine coolers may have lost their metal liners, not tremendously significant.

History: A wine cooler or cellaret was an important late eighteenth-century dining-room accessory, perhaps of less prestige than the Adam-type sideboard combination where the wine was stored in a pedestal cupboard. The octagonal or sarcophagus shapes are the most popular, and most are fairly plain with discreet decoration. Castors were an optional extra, and most wine coolers could be locked, which says something of the trust between master and servant. A shallow 'wine cooler' may not be what it appears, but an oyster bucket. The Victorians disdained the wine cooler, and its reign lasted about forty years.

Piece:	**OPEN ARMCHAIR**
Materials:	Gilded wood and cane
Dimensions:	3ft 6in high, 2ft 6in wide
Period:	*c*.1900
Value:	C a pair

POINTS TO LOOK FOR: The valuation is for this particular type of open armchair. Ordinary open armchairs can be bought for virtually nothing. This illustration is particularly interesting, for although made around 1900 it is in Regency style, eighty years earlier, and being of superb quality it could fool almost anybody. Look for decorative features that look out of keeping (you would have to examine genuine examples), and is the condition too good to be true? Rubbing of the gilding, expected after nearly two centuries, may be a plus.

HISTORY: Chairs with open arms, as opposed to upholstered, have co-existed with those without arms since early times, but they have a more impressive ancestry, deriving from the throne. In medieval times only the important sat on chairs; the inferiors sat on stools. Odd open armchairs, known as carvers, may be part of a dining-room set (there were two to a set). Among the most appealing open armchairs are country chairs, such as the Windsor and smoker's bow, but the form gave makers in the eighteenth century the opportunity to show off their skills and their ingenuity.

Piece:	**OVERMANTEL**
Material:	Gilt wood
Dimensions:	2ft 4in high, 4ft 3in wide
Period:	Late eighteenth century
Value:	B

POINTS TO LOOK FOR: With a piece of this complexity there is a lot to look out for, for these were executed in soft wood and then gilded, and it is likely that some of this gilding has worn off and been replaced, possibly by modern substitutes, even gold paint, any discrepancies in colour disguised. This particular overmantel has been stuck on top of a sideboard for a reason that is best known to the owner, but it was meant to be atop a fireplace and form an architectural whole. A degree of glass deterioration might be expected and is fairly acceptable.

HISTORY: The rococo movement, extravagance and curly nonsense without the grandeur of its predecessor, the baroque, was relatively short-lived, especially in Britain, and found its most potent manifestation in mirrors and the occasional piece of furniture ornament, often gratuitously grafted onto a sober traditional piece. Some overmantels were fitted with brackets for the display of china or with candlebranches. Temples, ruins, bridges, birds, mandarins and exotic figures were often incorporated. Chippendale has a great influence on rococo mirror design, and there were many pattern books issued in the 1750s.

Piece:	**PARTNER'S DESK**
Material:	Mahogany
Dimensions:	5ft wide
Period:	*c.*1825
Value:	D

POINTS TO LOOK FOR: Made without change for decade after decade, clues to age can be found from the type of handle. The brass ring handles are typical of this period. Earlier desks may have looped handles in the form of a 'swan's neck', later ones a knob or a pull-out in the form of a 'lion's head'. Value depends on size; this is a partner's desk, meaning that there are drawers (or cupboards) on both sides so that two people face each other while working. With hard usage, the leather top may be damaged or stained, and if it is seriously defective it is better to replace it than tart it up, not difficult, though real leather should be used and not a sustitute.

HISTORY: One of the most successful furniture designs, this type of desk is still extensively made. A variation is the kneehole desk, with a recessed cupboard between the pedestals, first made in walnut about 1710, and often used as a dressing table, some dressing tables being of that type. Early examples usually had bracket feet, or, less common, bun feet. Pedestal desks were often flush with the floor, or had concealed castors. Extra special eighteenth-century examples can top £15,000. Watch out for conversions from chests of drawers.

Piece:	**PEMBROKE TABLE**
Material:	Harewood and satinwood
Dimensions:	2ft 4in high, 2ft wide
Period:	*c*.1785
Value:	C

POINTS TO LOOK FOR: This is described as a Sheraton Pembroke table and is oval so that it is preferred to the rectangular. The spindly nature of the legs invites stress and incipient damage, and the spade feet (here unusually squat) need to be examined to see if they are original. Because the drop leaves, supported by slides, are small, chances of hinge damage and stress are lessened. Square legs are preferred to the later turned legs, and three hinges are better than two. The Edwardians made some very convincing Georgian-style Pembroke tables and have been known to be wrongly catalogued at auction.

HISTORY: The name Pembroke is obscure, and according to Sheraton, in his *Cabinet Dictionary* of 1803, was named after a 'lady who first gave orders for one of them, and who probably gave the first idea of such a table to the workmen.' Some say the first such table was ordered by Henry Herbert, Earl of Pembroke (1693–1751), doubtful, as it seems to have appeared about 1760. It was called 'spider-legged' because of the slender legs. The flaps can vary considerably in size, but often provided only a modest additional surface.

Piece: **PIANO STOOL**
Material: Mahogany
Dimensions: 1ft 10in high, 1ft 8in wide
Period: *c.*1880
Value A

POINTS TO LOOK FOR: This is not one of the better-quality stools. The wood is not of the best quality, the carving is dull and uninspiring, and the seat has been fitted with a ghastly covering, all of which reduce the value of this specific piano stool. The more sumptuous the carving the better, even if the upright tends to dominate the legs. The wind-up mechanism, a spiral screw, should work, and the metal elements should be crisp, not worn, for otherwise the top will slip down. There is often an inverted finial beneath the upright pillar between the legs, usually tripod. Buttoned leather is the favoured finish for the seat.

HISTORY: The wind-up piano stool was introduced in the Victorian period, and, unlike most stools, was not modelled on chair designs. The seat was usually round, but occasionally square, and as it was a perfectly designed object it was not capable of improvement. Its popularity coincided with the introduction of the upright cottage piano costing no more than £10, and as middle-class children were taught to play the piano as a matter of routine the adjustable-height stool was more than useful.

Piece:	**PLANT STAND**
Material:	Giltwood
Dimensions:	3ft 4in high, 2ft 4in wide
Period:	*c.*1810
Value:	D

POINTS TO LOOK FOR: When does furniture cease to be furniture? Is there a sharp defining line between furniture and miscellaneous items made of wood? This Regency oval jardiniere one would say is as much an item of furniture as a palm stand. A feature of this plant stand is that it is of gilt wood, and by its nature, gilding has a tendency towards damage and scuffing and it is always possible, though hardly with a very high value piece, that someone has renovated the gilding using cheap materials, even gold paint. The carving and finish should be crisp. The gilding should not clog any of the detail.

HISTORY: The Romans introduced gardening to Britain, and throughout the Dark Ages the religious orders maintained it. Its cultivation increased in the sixteenth century with the immigration of the Flemish escaping from persecution. The display of plants and flowers became a national fixation, especially after 1804 when the Horticultural Society was established. All kinds of furniture was evolved, some of it basic, some extremely elaborate as in this example with its echoes of the console table.

Piece:	**PRESS CUPBOARD**
Material:	Oak
Dimensions:	5ft 6in high, 4ft 10in wide
Period:	*c.*1650
Value:	C

POINTS TO LOOK FOR: As with all old oak, there are some fairly dubious examples about, reproductions and downright fakes. The press cupboard is one of several names for this piece of furniture; it can equally be described as a closed court cupboard. Although not a pretty piece of furniture, it has presence, especially if the carving is bold and not too finnicky – this may indicate a later 'improvement' by nineteenth-century carvers unable to resist a plain surface. Look for signs of wear, the smoothness that comes from centuries of waxing and polishing. Sometimes genuine old panels were inserted into a more modern cupboard, so look for subtle changes of colour in the wood.

HISTORY: One of the many definitions of 'press' is 'a cupboard or shelved closet or recess.' Press cupboards date from the sixteenth century, and the surface gives ample opportunity for not only carving but for inlay and the application of mouldings (decorative pieces stuck on to the body of the piece). Some press cupboards have all three. Most tall furniture has moulding round the top; some press cupboards did not, so mouldings have sometimes been added later.

Piece:	**'QUAINT' TABLE**
Materials:	Rosewood
Dimensions:	2ft 6in high, 3ft 2in wide
Period:	*c.*1880
Value:	D

Points to look for: This particular table was designed by the great pioneer of Art Furniture E.W. Godwin, but nevertheless belongs to a class of furniture called, often dismissively, quaint. A characteristic of quaint furniture is spindliness, and a multitude of legs, often without any structural purpose at all. Many quaint tables were ebonised, and are worth very little indeed, but this one is valuable because of the designer, the prestige wood, the curious central underhung pillar with struts to the legs, and the high quality of the turning and finish.

History: The London International Exhibition of 1862 had on view a variety of Japanese artefacts, and Godwin used Japanese furniture-design ideas to create a wholly new kind of furniture, sometimes called Anglo-Japanese, sometimes, especially when the Japanese connection is loose, Art Furniture. Godwin's work had a great effect on another adventurous designer, Charles Rennie Mackintosh (1868-1923), whose products command probably ten times as much as those of Godwin. Art Furniture has been described as a fad for a few fashion-conscious dandies.

Piece:	**RAIL-BACK ARMCHAIR**
Material:	Mahogany
Dimensions:	3ft high, 1ft 8in wide
Period:	*c.*1790
Value:	D set of six

Points to look for: The most vulnerable part of such a chair is the back, where the mid-bar could be most exquisitely made, often looking too frail for use. It will be noticed that the front legs are turned, the back legs square section, possibly slightly weakened by the slight curvature. It is always worth remembering that with chairs of this quality substitute legs may have been put in. The seat should be approximately 1ft 6in from the floor. A characteristic is the unusually high arms, not an eccentricity of this particular chair.

History: This type of chair, unassuming and unpretentious, was made for many years from the reign of George III onwards almost without change, and was suitable for revival in the early 1900s. An eighteenth-century example can often be differentiated from a later version by the wideness of the seat. The plain rectangular top rail was a favourite of makers, as it is of repairers or restorers,for it can be slotted neatly and easily into the uprights. The type of upholstered seat is known as over-stuffed, and although more elegant is more difficult to repair than the drop-in seats. This is covered with dralon; the quality deserves velvet.

Piece:	**REGENCY CHAISE LONGUE**
Materials:	Rosewood and beechwood with brass inlay
Dimensions:	5ft 4in long
Period:	*c.*1815
Value:	B

POINTS TO LOOK FOR: Because of its name the chaise longue has an almost mystical aura, and it is tempting for auctioneers to describe any settee or kind of lounging piece as one. The Regency version lacks the sinuous curves of its Victorian successor, and the rather stubby legs, usually known as urn shaped, are less desirable than cabriole amongst the buying public. Scroll ends are a decided plus. Original coverings are desirable but not common as furniture of this type has a good deal of wear and tear; replacement fabrics are acceptable when in keeping. This example has no back, and this perhaps makes it slightly less desirable.

HISTORY: The day couch whatever name it was travelling under, was a product of feminine sensibilities when an attack of the 'vapours' necessitating a lie-down was considered ladylike. Its introduction about 1770 also reflected the greater influence women exerted in the home from about 1770, and it was far more comfortable than the settees which were extended versions of the armchair or two-, three- or four-fold repeats of single chairs.

Piece:	**ROLL TOP DESK**
Material:	Rosewood
Dimensions:	4ft 5in high, 2ft 8in wide
Period:	*c.*1805
Value:	D

POINTS TO LOOK FOR: This is a superb example of a desk, predominantly intended for ladies, it could be described as a bonheur du jour, indeed often the descriptions are applied at the whim of the vendor. The fittings vary enormously, but this one has extra delights such as the elegant brass gallery and the exquisite turned pillars. There is no question of them being added in the interests of extra value, a point always worth bearing in mind. The solid roll top desk, unlike the commercial office roll top where slats are used, presents interesting problems. It was top of the range then and top of the range now.

HISTORY: This type of writing furniture was perhaps introduced from France and was just one of the many items made expressly for lady scribblers, one of the more outlandish being the Harlequin Pembroke table of Sheraton in which, through hidden and clever machinery a 'till', a concealed desk with drawers and pigeon holes, could be raised and lowered at will. A characteristic of all such furniture is that they are prestige pieces and not workaday furniture, useful to impress visitors. Such desks enjoyed a revival in the Edwardian period.

Piece:	**RUSSIAN DINING CHAIR**
Material:	Mahogany and brass
Dimensions:	3ft high, 1ft 10in wide
Period:	Late-eighteenth century
Value:	D set of four

POINTS TO LOOK FOR: It would need an expert to categorically state that these are Russian chairs, although people in the trade would decide that they are not English. There might be some dispute about their date; it could be argued that they are early-nineteenth century, the equivalent to Regency. An interesting question would be this: who would want to buy these chairs, high quality as they are, in preference to classic English chairs of the same period, except Russians? The curious design is not to everyone's taste.

HISTORY: Those who have read Tolstoy's *War and Peace* set in the period when these chairs were made will know that Russia was not just a place of mad tsars and downtrodden serfs. During the reign of Catherine the Great the decorative styles of France and England dominated Russian tastes, though native craftsmen (often serfs) introduced inlay of agate, ivory, jade, and mother-of-pearl and developed an individual style quite unlike that seen in the refined and subtle furniture of the best of the eighteenth-century furniture-makers of the west.

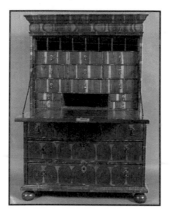

Piece:	**SECRETAIRE**
Material:	Oyster veneer and plum
Dimensions:	5ft 2in high, 3ft 6in wide
Period:	*c.*1690
Value:	D

POINTS TO LOOK FOR: Combinations of wood always present certain problems, mainly on aesthetic grounds, and there is often the feeling that the maker is feeling his way, especially when diverse woods are used. This secretaire is especially interesting in the use of vertical grain in the drawer fronts and oval figurations in the base and on the upper section beneath the cornice, with the light wood sections echoed. Normally the fall front would be closed, and there would not be a clash between the various types of handle. Considering its date, an imaginative piece.

HISTORY: Bureaux and secretaires evolved in a tortuous way from the simple portable writing boxes of the Middle Ages, and by the 1680–1700 period a suitable formula was being worked out. The lid concealing the writing section of a bureau has a sloping top. In America a bureau is known as a secretary. So there is little difference between a secretaire and the more popular bureau. In 1690 the interior drawers were basic; there was no attempt at ingenuity, and far more attention was devoted to interesting veneer on the exposed surfaces.

Piece:	**SEWING AND WRITING TABLE**
Material:	Satinwood with kingwood and ebony
Dimensions:	2ft 7in high, 1ft 10in wide
Period:	*c.*1790
Value:	C

POINTS TO LOOK FOR: Furniture of this quality usually comes from a specialist dealer or one of the top auction rooms, and if from the former has its own cachet and guarantee of quality. The rate of survival of such elegant eighteenth-century pieces is not high. During the Victorian age, when so much Georgian and Regency furniture was delegated to the servants' quarters, sewing and writing tables with long tapering legs and inbuilt fragility did not last long. There is always the possibility that furniture such as this has, over two hundred years, been metamorphosised into something else, perhaps losing its sewing bag and suffering conversion into a single-drawer table.

HISTORY: With the growing civilization and increasing role of women in society in the eighteenth century there was an increased emphasis on providing furniture for them, and them only, following the lead from France. Work tables of this type, with bags beneath, were not mentioned by Chippendale, though Sheraton evolved some ingenious designs. This table is in the style of George Seddon (1727–1801), one of the larger cabinet-makers employing about 400 men.

Piece:	**SIDEBOARD**
Material:	Mahogany and kingwood banding
Dimensions:	3ft 1in high, 6ft wide
Period:	*c.*1785
Value:	D

POINTS TO LOOK FOR: This type of sideboard is often regarded as a dressing table, but the end cupboards were used for keeping wine chilled. It was faithfully reproduced in the 1900s, and signs of wear, the gentle fading of old mahogany, the build-up of waxes and even grime, need to be studied to make certain that the example is eighteenth-century. Any inlay will show age better than a plain surface. It could be straight-fronted, bow, or serpentine and the more elaborate the better.

HISTORY: The sideboard derives from the court cupboard and the dresser, and in the eighteenth century it was a necessary and fashionable dining-room piece. The legs were usually six in number, often of tapering square section. In the early nineteenth century the side sections were extended downwards and fitted with squat feet. Ornamental columns were sometimes added. Sideboards became solid-doored cabinets, and the flattened-arch design of the 1840s held sway for decades. The sideboard with a large mirror at the back was followed by a gallery of eccentricities, often with iron and pewter fitments. Twentieth-century sideboards range from the refined to the truly awful.

Piece:	**SIDE TABLE**
Material:	Walnut
Dimensions:	2ft 3in high, 2ft 11in wide
Period:	*c.*1670
Value:	C

POINTS TO LOOK FOR: The older a piece is, the more difficult it is for the unscrupulous to summon up the signs of age in an imitation. It is also difficult to get the details right, for there is a curious ambivalence about Charles II furniture, when Dutch features were being grafted onto traditional English furniture styles. All cut-away or fretwork should be examined closely. In this instance, could the motif in the middle of the stretcher have been cut out to make the piece more interesting? It is a judgment the buyer must make. Barley-twist legs are very sturdy, but it is possible that these and the muffin-shaped feet may be bruised.

HISTORY: During the Restoration period tables of various woods were used indiscriminately for writing, tea, cards or merely to fill in floor spaces, and an assessment as to whether a certain table was intended for the side of a room may be purely personal, unless the one side is crudely finished when its destiny as a side table is assured. Woods were also mixed. In some tables where the tops were veneered with walnut the legs were sometimes of elm or fruitwood, so dissimilar but companionable woods are quite acceptable.

Piece:	**SMOKER'S TABLE**
Material:	Walnut
Dimensions:	2ft 7in high, 1ft 8in wide
Period:	Victorian
Value:	A

POINTS TO LOOK FOR: Although not readily apparent this table, termed a smoker's table though it could be used for any purpose, most probably for Berlin woolwork where the wool is kept in the lower stage, once had a spindled gallery around the top matching the one halfway up the column. This kind of thing can happen to any decorative form of furniture – something missing which is not obvious at first glance. The spindle holes have been filled in with plugs, but all such repairs can be discovered with a modicum of attention. The flat base with bun feet was popular from the 1830s onwards.

HISTORY: Despite its flat base, this table belongs to the same basic group as small tripods, derived from seventeenth-century candlesticks, which lent itself to many variations. A favourite device of Victorian makers was to give the top a 'pie-crust' edge, supposedly to stop cups and saucers or wine glasses from falling off. The visual advantage of a flat base over a tripod is that the central stem is longer and lends itself to more and often elaborate turning, especially of the baluster type as here, perfectly in keeping and seeming to indicate a fairly early type.

Piece:	**SOFA TABLE**
Material:	Rosewood and brass inlay
Dimensions:	2ft 4in high, 5ft wide
Period:	*c.*1815
Value:	D

POINTS TO LOOK FOR: Being one of the most desirable small pieces of furniture, and costing more than they are worth, sofa tables have been relentlessly faked. The end supports of fakes were taken from those of cheval mirrors which were very similar, sometimes identical. The example illustrated has a central pillared support standing on a flat base which in turn rests on feet, and the whole should be examined closely, especially the joints and where the end supports or the pedestal meet the top; look for irregularities, unexplained marks, and differences in wood colour. There are usually two drawers; versions with one long drawer are less desirable, and these have sometimes been altered. There are flaps at the long ends. Sofa tables were also made with stretchers.

HISTORY: The sofa table was introduced in the early years of the nineteenth century and meant to stand by a sofa. It was thus a ladies' piece, but it was also extensively used as an informal dining table. It came in all styles, from restrained perfection to examples with heavily carved central pillars and widely splayed ornate legs. Those with lyre end supports are especially valued.

Piece:	**SPECIMEN CHEST**
Material:	Mahogany
Dimensions:	6ft high, 2ft 8in wide
Period:	*c.*1910
Value:	B

Points to look for: As this piece is Edwardian, major defects are not acceptable. Any inlay and banding should be in good order, and each knob should be examined to ascertain there are no replacements. Take out every drawer, making sure each one slides easily, as these are specimen chests the drawers may have contained unspeakable things, leaving their mark. The drawers are graded in size, important to remember when putting them back; sometimes the differences between the drawers are very small, and it is easy to try and force the wrong one home.

History: The title Wellington chest is often given to specimen chests as illustrated, but this is wrong. Wellington chests are those with a hinged flap at the side which can be locked over the drawers, preventing them from being opened. As the Victorians were great collectors and hoarders, specimen chests were ideal for butterflies and their ilk. Many were of high quality and made in satinwood, walnut, and other superior woods, as well as carved oak around the 1880s. Others were ebonised with gilt-metal mounts. Some chests had false drawers, concealing a writing (or secretaire) section.

Piece:	**SPOON RACK**
Material:	Oak
Dimensions:	4ft high, 2ft 10in wide
Period:	*c.*1760
Value:	A

POINTS TO LOOK FOR: As with all furniture where fretwork is involved, it is important to make certain that all is as it should be, and not a modern machine-cut addition to something that might seem a trifle tame. Although conceived during the height of the mahogany fashion, this piece is of oak and unquestionably a country piece using fashionable Chippendale-derived motifs, not only the dentil moulding at the top and the tracery down the sides but the characteristic blind fretting at the base. The aprons beneath the slots for the spoons are an individual touch as well.

HISTORY: It would be idle to pretend that the spoon rack is a vitally important factor in the history of furniture, but it is interesting in that it represents an object the purpose of which is unlikely, bizarre, or obscure, unlike the porcelain spoon tray which was an invaluable tea-time accessory in the eighteenth century when tea-cups did not have saucers. It also occupies a place between standard and accepted items of furniture and treen, often droll and unusual objects made of wood. But there is an innocent charm about these well-made out-of-the way pieces.

Piece:	**STICK BACK CHAIR**
Materials:	Beech
Dimensions:	2ft 8in high, 1ft 4in wide
Period:	c.1920
Value:	A

POINTS TO LOOK FOR: Low-value chairs are more important for utility than their looks, and if the cost of recovering them, even in the basic manner, is greater than the value of the chairs their purchase should be reconsidered. Stick back chairs are among the most primitive, as the sticks can be whittled instead of turned on a lathe and as they slot into holes there are no construction difficulties. This chair is, of its kind, slightly above average though the covered top rail has the corners chamfered off so that the shape is neither one thing nor the other.

HISTORY: The stick or spindle has been used in chair manufacture for hundreds of years, and the principle was used in stools, especially the so-called milkmaid stools. The best-known spindle chair of all, the Windsor, was first recorded in 1724. The disposition of the spindles could be varied, the most attractive being to fan them out. About 1780 the spoon bit with a point was introduced, which meant that a deep hole could be bored without protruding through the other side of the wood, particularly useful for legs. A great advantage of stick backs is that broken spindles can be replaced by simple dowels.

Piece:	**TALLBOY**
Material:	Walnut
Dimensions:	5ft 7in high, 3ft 4in wide
Period:	*c.*1710
Value:	E

POINTS TO LOOK FOR: With all two-tier furniture, whether it is a chest on stand, chest on chest, or tallboy, it needs to be ascertained whether the two sections started life together. With a piece of this quality there is no question. In every way it looks 'right', from the proportions of the base and upper section to the figuration of the walnut. Queen Anne tallboys are unquestionably the province of the rich. They are sold by the upper echelons of the antique trade. They are rarely 'come across' and the fact that they come from a reputable source is a guarantee rarely less than cast-iron. A high-class dealer ceases to belong as soon as something suspect leaves his or her premises.

HISTORY: With the use of walnut veneer from about 1680 onwards the carcase was usually made of pine and the drawer linings were often made from wainscot oak imported from Scandinavia. This had an even grain. The oak linings of quality furniture were about a quarter of an inch thick; less significant furniture had thicker linings. The word tallboy for a chest on chest was introduced in 1676; it was applied to a chest atop a dressing table in 1769.

Piece:	**TAPESTRY-COVERED CHAIR**
Materials:	Mahogany
Dimensions:	3ft 5in high, 2ft 2in wide
Period:	*c.*1760
Value:	D

POINTS TO LOOK FOR: Original covering is a decided plus and can add markedly to the value of a piece of furniture especially when the back is covered as well. An expert on furniture is not necessarily an expert on tapestries as well, and even run-of-the-mill nineteenth-century tapestries, with their tendency to fade into a neutral brown, can look very old. A question that demands to be asked regarding expensive tapestry-covered furniture is what is happening beneath the covering? The woodwork in this Chippendale period chair is chunky and robust and a degree of bruising is acceptable.

HISTORY: In medieval times furniture was often simple and uncomplicated, but tapestries and other coverings and hangings were colourful and acted as a foil to the simple oak. Tapestries or fragments of tapestries exist from the twelfth century, and a fair number survive from the fourteenth and fifteenth. In the eighteenth century tapestry-making in Flanders thrived, with the French in strong competition, and Beauvais and Aubusson specialised in the production of furniture covers, and it is likely that the tapestry on this chair is French.

Piece:	**TIP-UP CENTRE TABLE**
Materials:	Amboyna and marquetry
Dimensions:	2ft 5in high, 3ft 10in diameter
Period:	*c.*1843
Value:	E

POINTS TO LOOK FOR: There are really no points to look for in this marvellous table, made by the cabinet-maker E.H. Baldock of London, but in lesser tables attention must be given to the quality of the marquetry, possible warping, weakness in the hinges, signs of stress on the central support, bubbling on the veneer of the main sections of wood (and indications of bubble-removal), and, where the feet jut out, bruising and possible damage, less so in a small table such as this but probable in the larger tip-up table used for card games such as loo where damage to feet is caused by sitters' shoes or boots.

HISTORY: Round tables, with and without a tip-up facility which could be used for dining, games, and as occasional tables became very popular from the early nineteenth century as they afforded craftsmen a wonderful opportunity to display their skills in marquetry, mosaic, inlay of semi-precious stones and the use of exotic woods. Some of the highest quality tables are known as saloon tables. This table was made to commemorate the visit of King Louis Philippe (1773–1850) of France in 1844 (a pity he had to flee his country as 'Mr Smith' in 1848 when the mob rose against him).

Piece:	**TRAY-TOP POT HOLDER**
Material:	Mahogany
Dimensions	2ft 6in high, 1ft 9in wide
Period:	Late-eighteenth century
Value:	A

POINTS TO LOOK FOR: These are simple basic items of furniture because they were bedside furniture, and not meant to be seen by outsiders. Ornament is kept to the minimum, so it is quite easy to check that any inlay or banding is in good condition. The tray surrounds are of a fairly simple form, but try to ascertain that what might have been a plain edging has not been meddled with at a later stage to make it more decorative. The drop handles as shown are in keeping; if knobs have been fitted they indicate a later date.

HISTORY: Other names for the pot holder are the night table and the commode. The commode, strictly speaking, is the French name for a chest of drawers, but in Britain it has been colloquially used since the eighteenth-century to denote a repository for a chamber pot. Nineteenth-century examples could be very ordinary, and could be fitted with steps (these can be confused with bed steps, helping someone to climb into bed). There are also versions in the form of a cylinder or elongated octagon with a marble top. These are now used as general-purpose stands, as plumbing and the flushable lavatory made commodes obsolescent, if not quite obsolete.

Piece:	**TRIPOD TABLE**
Material:	Oak
Dimensions:	2ft 4in high, 1ft 6in wide
Period:	Eighteenth century
Value:	A

POINTS TO LOOK FOR: There can hardly be a simpler piece of furniture, and the main variation between country tripods is the method of fixing the top to the upright. In this case there is a batten, which may or may not indicate that it was once a tip-top and has been adapted. The dating is speculative as such tables were made for a very long period. It is often said, with so many old tripod tables not so old as they look, that the width of the top should be the same as that of the feet, but this is not reliable. The legs of all tripod tables should be checked at the point where they abut the column.

HISTORY: The traditional tripod table probably derives from the candlestick which was introduced to Britain at the time of the Restoration of Charles II and was adapted over the years to provide support for almost any object. Wine tables often had a spindle gallery around the top, and superior tripod tables had a 'birdcage' beneath the top, a distinctive method of fixing top to column, and such tables carry a premium even though it was a purely structural device as the birdcage itself is not on view unless one looks for it.

Piece:	**TWO-PART CHEST**
Materials:	Oak and snakewood
Dimensions:	3ft 1in high, 3ft 3in wide
Period:	*c.*1660
Value:	C

POINTS TO LOOK FOR: The last flourish of oak was quite spectacular, and some of the furniture may strike one as odd, so different to the earlier furniture. Geometric panelled decoration was mitred, marked by strong projections in the centre, and there was a fascination with not only woods such as zebra wood, partridge wood, and, as here, snake wood (red with dark brown spots) but also bone and mother-of-pearl, all used as inlay against traditional oak. The two-part chest is not the most useful of objects; it can be seen as a transitional piece.

HISTORY: The storage chest took many years to transform itself into a chest of drawers, and there were a number of half-way houses. Oak inlaid with exotic woods was a relatively short-lived phenomenon, made old-fashioned overnight by Dutch-influenced floral marquetry introduced about 1670, which in turn fell from favour except in the case work of long-case clocks. The technique in which a thin layer of veneer was laid on a carcase of unimportant wood was totally different to the painstaking inlay into the oak body. One of the turning points of furniture history.

Piece:	**TWO-PIECE FOLDING SCREEN**
Material:	Silk on wooden open frame.
Dimension:	5ft 6in wide (opened), 6ft high.
Period:	Late-nineteenth century.
Value:	B

POINTS TO LOOK FOR: Elegant wooden framework, mahogany being the favourite wood, and the quality of the decoration (sometimes high-quality paintings) is more important than anything else, even if the frame is ornate. If the screen is of leather, make certain that it is not deteriorating (indicated by a pinkness known as red rot). If of lacquer ensure that any ivory decorations glued on are all there. Screens decorated with scraps are later than the mid-nineteenth century; often clumsy attempts have been made to remove some of the scraps.

HISTORY: A covered hinged frame, in two or more sections, used from the Middle Ages to prevent draughts or split up a room, and becoming increasingly elaborate from the sixteenth century when lacquered screens were imported from Japan, and later copied. Lacquer screens were often decorated with flat ivory carvings. Screens were sometimes made of leather, often elaborately tooled, and in the nineteenth century screens of wood or covered with fabric were sold plain and decorated by the owner with scraps (cut-out pictures). Lacquer screens reappeared in the 1920s. These are of modest value.

Piece:	**TYROLEAN ARMOIRE**
Material:	Pine
Dimensions:	6ft 6in high, 5ft 2in wide
Period:	1791
Value:	B

Points to look for: The construction of such pieces is often basic, and joints are sometimes crude, with the maker relying on the weight of the structure to hold it all together. If there is a cornice fitted, removal of it may cause the armoire to fall apart. The quality of the painting is often naive, and some pine dealers imagine that they can price up ambiguous wardrobes by painting pictures on them which they then sandpaper down or partly strip. Locks and hinges sometimes provide a clue to age; strap hinges are common, but these can be convincingly aged.

History: The armoire will not be found in books on English furniture, and is essentially a cupboard of somewhat monumental character, often richly and extravagantly carved, sometimes with a strong local character, or painted, a speciality of Bavarian and Austrian examples. To confuse matters, the word is occasionally applied to an upright or drop-front secretaire which looks like a cupboard when closed. An armoire á deux corps is a French name for a piece of architectural furniture consisting of two cupboards, each with two doors, the upper cupboard being recessed.

Piece:	**URN ON STAND**
Material:	Mahogany
Dimensions:	7ft 3in total height
Period:	*c*.1810
Value:	D set of two

POINTS TO LOOK FOR: Urns on stands are uncommon, and although the lids of the urns seem to be detachable it is idle to speculate on their contents, if any. Whereas in standard pieces of furniture it is possible to get away with slightly woolly carving, in urns of this type, which act in a setting as exclamation marks, the carving has to be absolutely crisp. The urn mounts are of bronze, and between the base and the urn there is a square of marble or marbled wood, which may or may not be out of place. Metal extras should always be examined with extra attention to ascertain their credibility or the possibility of repair; bronze sometimes acquires a patina, not really compatible with mahogany.

HISTORY: The urn, where the Romans kept the ashes of the dead, was one of the key icons of the Neo Classical movement of the eighteenth century, and it continued to have an almost mystical appeal throughout the nine-teenth century perhaps because of the universal fascina-tion with death and its accessories. The urn-shape was also popular in silver when serving tea, chocolate, or coffee. Sometimes vases were misleadingly called urns.

Piece:	**VITRINE**
Material:	Tulipwood and gilt metal
Dimensions:	5ft high, 2ft wide
Period:	*c*.1910
Value:	C a pair

POINTS TO LOOK FOR: Vitrines can be extremely elaborate, comprising mirrors, often oddly shaped, as well as expanses of glass. This vitrine is French, and the hand-painted decoration is typical. Make certain such decoration is hand-painted and not a transfer print, quite easy to do by passing the finger tip over. A slight irregularity of surface indicates hand-painting. Or use a magnifying glass and look for brush marks. Vitrines are too elaborate to fake, so it is a question of checking the condition. See that any glass is firmly held in place. Check the legs – they often look too flimsy for the weight they carry.

HISTORY: The vitrine is essentially an auctioneer's term for a large display cabinet or china cabinet, which developed in the nineteenth century from the side cabinet to hold the multitudes of odds and ends the Victorians accumulated. There was no standard model, and until recently many were dismissed as monstrosities, often based on French models which were less monstrous because they were French. They were made in all woods. Edwardian mahogany vitrines, vaguely based on eighteenth-century themes, are often elegant and grossly undervalued.

Piece:	**WALL MIRROR**
Material:	Gilt wood and gesso
Dimensions:	3ft 11in high, 2ft 2in wide
Period:	c.1745
Value:	C

Points to look for: Mirror glass was very difficult to make and expensive, and thinner than modern glass; to find out the thickness of mirror glass hold a finger nail against the surface. A degree of speckling is probable. If it is a fine frame, resilvering of the mirror glass is acceptable. The frame is coated with gesso, plaster and glue size, very vulnerable to damp, easily broken off into chalky fragments. The more intricate frames had gesso spun out from the surface on wire.

History: Until the seventeenth century glass mirrors were imported from Venice. Frames were large to make the mirrors appear bigger. In the late seventeenth century frames were veneered, walnut and olive being favourite woods. Lacquer was also used, but gesso was the most spectacular, with cresting, shells, plumes, and other motifs. Gesso declined, carved gilt wood being preferred. Cheaper mirror glass brought in great architectural set-pieces, often asymmetrical, sometimes in the Chinese style. From about 1760 mirrors were decorated with motifs such as husks, vases, honeysuckle, rams' heads, ox skulls and sphinxes to fit in with Neoclassical ideas.

Piece:	**WELSH DRESSER**
Material:	Oak
Dimensions:	6ft 5in high, 6ft 2in wide
Period:	Eighteenth century
Value:	E

POINTS TO LOOK FOR: This dresser is from Montgomeryshire, and is an example of what matters and what does not matter in a piece of this age and quality. The absence of several of the drop handles is of no concern. The buyer will provide his or her own, perhaps rooting around for genuine handles or buying good-quality replacements. Two of the original feet have been replaced by blocks of wood without any attempt to cover up. The difference in the colouration of the wood at the back of the shelves indicates replacement, acceptable because it is an old replacement.

HISTORY: Being essentially a provincial piece of furniture, the dresser was constructed by men, perhaps not even cabinet-makers, not acquainted with current London fashions. Montgomeryshire was more remote than other parts of Wales where coal mining had introduced a degree of cosmopolitanism. However, echoes of Neo-classicism have crept into this dresser in the side supports of the shelving, though the apron harks back to tradition. A characteristic of many dressers of the period is the low platform base, though sometimes floor-level stretchers are preferred.

Piece:	**WILLIAM AND MARY CHAIR**
Material:	Walnut and cane
Dimensions:	5ft high
Period:	*c.*1690
Value:	D set of six

POINTS TO LOOK FOR: The most vulnerable parts of these chairs, which are also known as Anglo-Dutch, is the caning and the cost of recaning is not cheap. It is difficult to disguise damage on caning, unlike straw seating. Turning to the wood, the most vulnerable parts are the bulbous knees and feet which, if badly knocked, can split across the grain. The finials on the top of the back uprights are also susceptible to damage. As the wood is walnut these chairs are subject to woodworm. It may be dead woodworm; if there are woodworm holes, tap the chair against a hard surface and see if any sawdust falls out.

HISTORY: From the return of Charles II from exile continental influences on furniture became important, and there was an attempt to reconcile British styles with those from abroad, especially Holland and France. Fashionable French furniture, far more elegant than British, had long been imported. Oak was decreed unfashionable and walnut took over as the preferred wood. The late-seventeenth chair was transitory. Its gimmicks such as the arch beneath the seat were soon discarded, and the ungainly ornamentation pared down.

Piece:	**WILLIAM AND MARY CHEST ON STAND**
Materials:	Walnut
Dimensions:	4ft 7in high, 3ft 2in wide
Period:	*c.*1700
Value:	C

POINTS TO LOOK FOR: The chest on stand was a design aberration, for the stand itself was often too flimsy to take the weight of the chest and there was a busy trade amongst journeyman carpenters in supplying replacement stands. Many of these replacement stands are almost contemporary with the original and have thus acquired the appropriate signs of age, though possibly indications of inferior quality to the chest may be present. The example illustrated, with characteristic cabriole legs and pad feet, is described as 'restored', which may indicate a degree of uncertainty.

HISTORY: There was an great variety in the designs of chests of drawers; most people stored their clothes flat and folded rather than hung. Furniture of the William and Mary period was strongly influenced by Dutch and French taste, and the surfaces presented by drawer fronts was often irresistible, veneered in a variety of woods. Holly, box, pear and sycamore on a walnut ground were popular. By about 1700 the construction of chests of drawers was becoming more delicate, with finer dovetailing and greater attention to detail.

Piece:	**X-FRAME TABLE**
Material:	Mahogany
Dimensions:	2ft 8in high, 3ft 2in wide
Period:	*c.*1920
Value:	A

POINTS TO LOOK FOR: With X-frame tables there is always a downwards-and-outwards pressure on the legs, especially if they are exceptionally slender as here, though the turned stretchers help to spread the weight of the top. This is a tip-up table, and although the simple mechanism may be working well there is always the chance that over the years the blocks which determine where the legs should meet the top have become worn. The top will still be supported but it may well be off the horizontal. Such tables usually have hard usage and have got damaged on the top. Faults in mahogany are easily remedied.

HISTORY: The folding X-chair and stool were known in ancient Egypt and Rome with leather or skin seats. In the Renaissance stools were solid with the cross members carved, and it remained a popular form, with Thomas Hope a convincing practitioner of the type in the eighteenth century. The X-frame table is very much the poor relation, for when not in use and folded it is inclined to look poor and mean, unlike the tripod tip-up. X-frame collapsible tables are small, as large ones cannot be easily assembled by one person.

Woods
Used
In
Furniture

ACACIA
Hard, yellow with brown figuration, used as inlay, banding and stringing, regarded as a cheaper substitue for tulip wood.

ALDER
A 'country' wood, pale fleshy colour, curly markings.

AMBOYNA
Prestige wood from West Indies, a rich lightish brown with a prominent figure.

APPLE
Hard, reddish-brown and close-grained, sometimes stained and used as a subsitute for ebony. Can be confused with pearwood.

ASH
Greyish, heavy, springy, subject to woodworm and, though frequently used in the past, has often not survived. Could be used a a veneer, and for drawer linings, but most often is seen in country furniture.

BEECH
Speckled, light brown, soft, liked by woodworm, but cheap and used on carcass furniture and all articles, such as tables where a true, smooth and durable surface is wanted. The grain is so dense that it is difficult to see the yearly growth rings.

BIRCH Light yellowish-brown, soft, cheap, used as a substitute for satinwood and for country furniture.

Boxwood
Pale yellow, no grain worth speaking of, used for stringing, banding and inlay, especially on early oak. Greatly used in the manufacture of woodwind instruments.

BRAZILWOOD
Red, richly marked and hard, can be confused with mahogany but mainly used for inlay.

CALAMANDER
Brown, mottled and streaked with black, imported from Ceylon and used from about 1780 for inlay, banding, and stringing.

CEDAR
Cheap, reddish-brown, not unlike mahogany and used for chest and interior work from the middle of the eighteenth century.

CHERRY
Pale, maturing to a fairly strong red, not unlike mahogany but with a closer grain, and used as inlay etc.

CHESTNUT
Horse chestnut is almost white, used for drawer linings. Sweet chestnut is reddish, quite hard, used for country furniture or as cheap substitute for other woods in inlay and banding.

COROMANDEL
Utterly distinctive, yellow and black striped, imported from India and much used for flashy inlay and banding.

CYPRESS
An uncommon wood from the Middle East, reddish, close grained, known as moth-resistant and used in fairly early chests and other containers.

DEAL
Pine, straight grained, cheap, used for carcase furniture.

Ebony

Black or dark brown, heavy, close-grained, used as inlay from the sixteenth century, imitated using stained pearwood and applewood.

Elm

Brown, with blackish figure, subject to woodworm but widely used by country makers though burr elm makes agreeable veneer.

Harewood

Fancy name for sycamore stained grey-green, used for inlay, banding and stringing.

Hickory

Widely used by American colonists. Hard, sturdy, durable, and with a springiness found also in the ash.

Holly

Hard, white, and with a close grain. One of the first contrasting woods used for inlay against oak.

Kingwood

A Brazilian prestige wood, brown and black, striated like rosewood and used as a veneer as well as for inlay from the seventeenth century. Favoured by the French.

Laburnum

As plain veneer, browny-yellow with streaks. The branches make a pleasant oyster blackish-brown veneer.

Lignum Vitae

A West Indian wood, brown with black streaks, a strange wood and very hard indeed – less air (13 per cent) than in any other wood, used as a veneer, inlay, and in the solid.

Lime

Whitish-yellow, close-grained, loved by wood carvers and uncommon in fine furniture.

MAHOGANY

There are three basic types: 'Spanish' or 'Cuban' from the West Indies used for classic eighteenth-century furniture; 'Honduras', lighter in colour, pinkish from the late eighteenth century; 'Canary', lighter still, yellowish-brown, regarded as inferior.

MAPLE

Light yellow, used as vener and in marquetry, while the 'slices' from branches form the celebrated 'bird's-eye' maple adored by the Victorians.

OAK

Oak used before the middle of the seventeenth century has become very dark or mid-brown, eighteenth-century oak as used by country makers is lighter, with distinctive straggling yellow rays. Usually used in the solid, though oak veneer exists. Oak was often used for drawer linings and carcase furniture. Bog oak, oak preserved in peat, is nearly black, as is fumed oak, oak exposed to ammonia fumes, favoured by the Victorians. Clapboard is imported oak, softer, paler, and with a finer grain than the native tree. Oak is resistant to woodworm.

OLIVE

Greenish with dark streaking, hard and close-grained, somewhat similar to yew and used in marquetry, occasionally in veneers. Olive branches make a good oyster veneer.

PADOUK

A Burmese wood akin to rosewood, reddish with a blackish figure, heavy, first imported about 1730 and used in the solid, popular in Anglo-Indian type furniture.

PARTRIDGEWOOD

A rare wood from Brazil, streaky red and brown (imaginatively seen as like partridge feathers), used from the seventeenth century but not in quantity.

PEAR
Yellowish-brown with little grain, often stained to imitate ebony, a favourite of country makers, ocasionally used as an inlay (most woods were).

PLANE
White and close-grained, used by country makers and as a substitute for beech, but not an easily identified wood.

PLUM
Yellowish-red, used mainly by country makers, ocasionally as inlay from the seventeenth century.

POPLAR
Greyish and hard, used as an inlay but not extensively.

PURPLEWOOD
A fancy wood from Brazil, the purple turning to brown used as inlay and veneer. Hard and heavy it is not unlike rosewood.

ROSEWOOD
The prestige wood of the Regency and Victorian periods, coming in a range of shades from hazel to deep brown with black often dramatic streaking, hard, even-grained and good to carve.

SABICU
A rare Cuban wood often taken to be mahogany and used in the early eighteenth century – but not often.

SATINWOOD
Yellowish, used in the solid and as veneer, inlay, and other decorative methods, perhaps the favourite wood for such purposes in the late-eighteenth and early-nineteenth century with its fine plain grain and unobtrusive quality.

SNAKEWOOD
Red with dark brown spots and markings (like a snake's skin), used in the eighteenth century as inlay and as a veneer.

SYCAMORE
White with a fleck, close-grained, easily stained, used as a veneer and for inlay and banding.

TEAK
Deep reddish-brown, strong, durable, often use in Colonial furniture where teak was the native wood. Because of its strength greatly used in campaign furniture.

THUYAWOOD
African wood of the 'bird's eye' type used in eighteenth century as a veneer etc.

TULIPWOOD
Yellow-brown with reddish stripes from Brazil, mainly used from the late-eighteenth century for banding.

WALNUT
English walnut is golden-brown with dramatic dark patterning, and the branches much used for oyster veneer. Walnut especially popular 1660–1740, but revived in the Victorian period. Black walnut known as Virginia walnut was also grown in England, and was considerably darker. Italian, Spanish and French walnut was lighter with a less pronounced figure.

WILLOW
Little used except when stained black and used as a substitute for ebony.

YEW
Very hard, reddish-brown, much used by country makers and prized by London makers for the fine effect from pollarded trees (burr yew).

ZEBRAWOOD

Named after the stripes of a zebra and imported from Guiana, a spectacular brown and dark striped wood used as a veneer from the late-eighteenth century.

Furniture
Decoration

Decoration can be applied to furniture in many ways; the wood can be carved, engraved or gouged. The base wood can be inset with other woods or materials such as brass, it can be painted, varnished, waxed, or overlaid with a thin sheet of contrasting wood (veneering). This veneer can be plain, relying on the natural figure of the wood, or it can be made into shapes (marquetry). Square edges can be made smooth or round with mouldings; these can be carved into the actual wood, or applied, using glue, nails, or even screws. If wood is likely to get scuffed, vulnerable parts can be protected with mounts of metal. These mounts, usually brass or brass-like (ormolu) can also be applied as pure decoration. Decorative pieces such as plaques can be stuck on suitable plain surfaces - much used on the continent, rather less so in Britain until the nineteenth century.

Some articles of furniture, such as chairs, lend themselves to extensive decoration and variation. The shape of a piece of furniture can be determined by need or fashion. Many of these styles are eye-catching, but have structural disadvantages, because of the manner in which the grain of the wood runs, with the possibilty of the wood splitting with the grain. Decorative motifs reflect current fads, and there is a type of decoration where the object is to break up a boring plain surface and nothing more.

Among the motifs used have been:

knotted ribbons and bows

rising sun ornament

fan

roundel

fluting

scroll

inverted pear shape

animals' heads

reeding

fruit, flowers and foliage (known as swags)

half moon

lyre

quarter-round and half-round sections

tooth shaped

egg shapes with arrowheads or triangles

ogee (two curves)
animals' feet (for chair legs etc)
pear-drop
husk (wheat ear)
herring-bone
lattice
cabochon (design of polished uncut diamond)
ball (used for feet, sometimes with a claw)
bead moulding (like row of beads)
bell flower
bobbin
chequer (chess-board pattern)
club foot
spade foot (tapered square section)
split baluster (baluster cut in half)
cock beading (half-round moulding)
concave frieze (inward sloping)
convex frieze (outward sloping, like cushion)
shell
cupid's bow
anthemion (honeysuckle)
amorini (cupids)
acanthus leaf
guilloche (interlaced ribbon enclosing circles)
Prince of Wales feathers
palmette (branching palm tree)
vase
arcaded (a series of arches)
diaper (diamond shapes often with dots inside)
gadrooning (repetitive curved shapes usually convex)
baluster turning
(lathe-executed bulging pear shapes of varying sizes)

Credits

Bliss Furniture, Camelford, Cornwall 50, 74

Robin Fenner, Auction Rooms, Tavistock, Devon 40, 89, 97

Gothick Dream, Arthoy Hall, Gwynedd, Wales 73

Sean Hickey, Rooms, West Street, Ashburton, Devon 29, 31

Wakelin and Linfield, 10 New Street, Petworth, Sussex 38, 47, 52, 55, 57, 69, 70, 75, 88, 105, 108, 112, 114, 125

Witney Antiques (member of the BADA), 96-100 Corn Street, Witney, Oxon 39, 43, 45, 68, 78, 79, 85, 92, 106, 116, 119

All other illustrations are from the author's collection